Captivated
by CHRIST

Captivated by CHRIST

Wesley Nelson

CHRISTIAN LITERATURE CRUSADE
Fort Washington, Pennsylvania 19034

CHRISTIAN LITERATURE CRUSADE
Fort Washington, Pennsylvania 19034

CANADA
1440 Mackay Street, Montreal, Quebec

GREAT BRITAIN
The Dean, Alresford, Hampshire

AUSTRALIA
P.O. Box 91, Pennant Hills, N.S.W. 2120

SBN 87508-433-8

Introduction

I KNEW I OUGHT to be a better Christian. I also knew that there were certain things that would make me a better Christian. It must all be by the grace of God. But the grace of God must be received by faith, and my faith was weak. I understood that my faith must be strengthened by feeding on the Word of God, but reading the Bible was becoming an increasingly difficult chore. It would help if I prayed more fervently for the Spirit to enlighten the Scriptures, but when I prayed my mind wandered. I needed to discipline myself, but I lacked the will power. If I were a better Christian, I would read my Bible more and pray better, my faith would be strengthened, and I would be able to exercise more self-discipline. But how could I become a better Christian when I could not do the things that would make me a better Christian? I was caught in a vicious circle. I was preaching release and I dared not admit, even to myself, that I was a slave to religious bondage. I preached victorious living with fervor, urging people to claim the victory by faith. Personally I never felt very victorious; but I told myself that victory is not by feeling, but by faith. Yet, my faith was weak, and I often found it difficult to believe I had the victory. In fact, I obviously didn't have it. In times of emergency, when I needed it most, my faith was weakest, and my victory was gone.

It is a terrifying sensation to have one's religion fail him. Yet, for me, it was the best thing that could have happened, for, when everything else failed, Christ stepped in, and He did not fail. None of the theological truths changed, but a new significance was injected into them. I had preached a Gospel for sinners. Now I discovered that Christ was not asking me to come to Him as a prayed-up, Bible-loving, God-honoring, fully-consecrated, victorious-living, witnessing, successful soul-winning Christian. He was inviting me to come just as a sinner. It was a simple thing, but it was like throwing open the windows of a stuffy room.

For awhile I was confused about the Bible. I had always interpreted the Bible as calling Christians to advanced accomplishments and to lofty achievements. There was Christian growth, the resurrection life, dying to sin, identification with Christ, victorious living, consecration, the Spirit-filled life, etc. Did not all this require one to be something more than just a sinner?

I began to read the New Testament from the viewpoint of a sinner. To my surprise, it opened to me with new clarity. One night, as I was re-reading the Epistle to the Romans, I saw for the first time that the cross of Christ was central throughout the entire epistle, and that Paul was dealing with the same subject in the sixth, seventh and eighth chapters as he was in the third chapter. The sixth chapter of Romans, with its complicated references to dying with Christ, immediately dissolved into simplicity when I saw it through the eyes of a mere sinner. I do not know how many times I read the Epistle to the Romans that night, but dawn was breaking in the east before I could force myself to lay it aside.

Still, I was discovering no new truth. These were the things I had known since my youth. The difference was, that whereas previously I had been trying to find a way to Christ, now Christ, Himself, became the Way. It was the Shepherd who was leading me to the fountains of life.

In this book I have tried to reflect the simplicity of some of these things. In some places I have found it impossible to be as clear as I would like. The more complicated portions, however, are the places where I am trying to back out of the theological snarls that result from reading something into the Bible that will make us out to be something more than sinners.

To have a true storybook ending, this tale should conclude with an account of how much more fruitful my life and ministry have become as a result of these refreshing experiences. I do not say that this has been the case. I feel more like the little group of disciples in the hour when the multitudes were turning from Jesus, and He asked them if they, too, would go away. "Lord," they replied, "to whom shall we go? You have the words of eternal life."

I am writing of that which has captivated my soul. Whether I see any fruit or not; whether it seems to be a blessing to others or not; whether it is accepted, ignored, or rejected, I cannot turn back. This is not something I have apprehended out of the great storehouse of Truth. It has apprehended me. If this is not the way, then, for me, there is no way. I have nowhere else to turn. To whom should I go?

I wish to express my appreciation to those who, by their suggestions and criticisms, have assisted me in the preparation of this book. I have been greatly dependent on their help to clarify several of the ideas which are discussed.

The Biblical quotations which are used are from the Revised Standard Version. They are used by permission of the copyright owners, the National Council of the Churches of Christ in the U.S.A.

W. W. N.

CONTENTS

Introduction 5

Foreword 11

Chapter One: The Good News 15

Chapter Two: The Teachings of Jesus 29

Chapter Three: The Dominion of Sin 31

Chapter Four: What the Cross Really Means 41

Chapter Five: Applying the Cross to Christian Living 55

Chapter Six: The Flesh and the Spirit 73

Chapter Seven: The Christian's Warfare 93

Chapter Eight: A New Relationship 105

Chapter Nine: Jesus is Lord! 119

FOREWORD TO THE 1974 EDITION

I love this book. My own copy which I have had since the first edition came out in 1956 is heavily underlined throughout. Some time ago when I turned back to it after the passage of some years, it was to find that some of the insights into the message of grace which I had proclaimed all over the world had been gained initially from this book. God had made them so much a part of my life and thinking that I had almost forgotten how they came to me in the first place and how much I owed to Wesley Nelson for their rediscovery.

I not only love this book, but I love the man who wrote it. He is my brother; we have met as sinners at the foot of the Cross of Jesus. And I value the all-too-infrequent times when we are able to link up again in personal fellowship. Although we are separated by a big ocean and a big continent, that fellowship has remained, for I know where to find him and I trust he knows where to find me—still in the place of the sinner at the foot of the Cross on redemption ground, the ground of grace.

The fact that this book takes a new look at the Epistle to the Romans, especially at chapters six to eight, is important to me. Years ago when the Lord first led me into full-time evangelistic work in England, I had a well-developed doctrine of sanctification, of the victorious life, and it was based on these chapters. I will not deny it—God used the aspect of reckoning myself dead to sin that Christ might live in me to help me; and that, very decisively, as it seemed then. But I have to confess that later I lost the blessing of it, and that, however much I sought to reckon and claim by faith my position in Christ, I failed to regain that which I had lost—and yet I had to continue to do public evangelistic work. It was in this condition that I was confronted with the simple, disconcerting message of revival, as it came to me through those who had come out of revival in East Africa. It seemed just a restatement of the message of the gospel which I had been preaching to those who were not yet Christians, and I was puzzled to know how it fitted in with my doctrine of sanctification. Finally I consented to stop arguing (and I did argue!) and come, as a sinner on specific things the Spirit had revealed, to the Cross of Jesus to be cleansed —and I began to "strike oil" again. I decided to rest my doctrine of sanctification and my expositions of these chapters and go on with just those things that the Lord was making currently living to me. Somehow I felt that those chapters must mean something simpler and more workable than I had made them to be and they must be in line with the new experience of grace I had entered into. I feel now that in these later years God has led me back to those chapters, but through a different door. I have discovered that they are nothing more than another and fuller statement of the grace that had met me when I began to come as a defeated evangelist to the Cross. It has been my joy to find others who have likewise found new light on these chapters, Wesley Nelson among them. His book has further helped me to rid myself of "the theological snarls that result from reading something into the Bible that will make us out to be something more than sinners," to quote his own words. To imagine that such an emphasis on the grace of God for sinners is morbid and negative is the very opposite of the truth. It is the law that makes us morbid; grace makes us free.

For all these reasons I warmly welcome this new edition and would recommend it warmly to those with hungry hearts.

ROY HESSION

London, England 1973

CHAPTER ONE

The Good News

"**I**'M AFRAID," he said, "that you're wasting your time on me. I suggest that you just mark me down as a lost soul."

He was not speaking facetiously. I knew him well enough to know that he was not merely trying to put me off. He was a sincere man. On several occasions I had tried to tell him what Christ could do for him. He never resented these "religious conversations," as he called them, and he often brought up the subject himself. We were on good terms, but he seemed to be completely and hopelessly blind to spiritual truth.

I can remember how he sat, rather dejectedly, stoically resigned to his fate. The smoke from his cigarette curled upward toward the ceiling of his living room as he told me of his losing battle with unbelief. He knew the teachings of the Bible. He was able to repeat without a flaw the way to "accept Christ as your Saviour." He was a man with religious interests; he often attended church, but he was in a starless night of spiritual darkness.

"I have tried to believe," he said, "but I can't. I have read the Bible, but it doesn't speak to me. I have tried to pray, but prayer is completely meaningless. I have tried to repent, but I can't get myself to feel repentant. I have tried to accept Christ as my personal Saviour, but nothing happens. If I could get myself to believe that something would happen, it probably would, but I can't. It may do for others, but not for me. I have resigned myself to being a lost soul."

It is for men like him that I am writing. Strangely, there are Believers who face problems quite similar to his, to whom this will also apply. These are the believers for whom life has reached a stalemate because they lack the faith to go on. Christian living for them is a wilderness experience, with a refreshing oasis only here and there. "Rivers of living water" and "the abundant life" are only religious expressions to them. They may have listened to sermons and expositions on "the deeper life," but none of the formulas seem to work. They seem to lack whatever it takes to benefit by what God seems to have promised. So they resign themselves to the proposition that Christian experience for them cannot be as refreshing as it is for other "more spiritual" Christians.

Both my unbelieving friend and these believers are blocked by obstacles. He is prevented from entering the gates of the Christian life. They, having entered, are prevented from going on. There is good news for both. It is the good news of Christ who is both the door to life and the way of life. Both the door and the way lead through every conceivable obstacle.

I would like to think of my unbelieving friend and these believers as forming a little circle who will consider, in simple, non-theological terms, what really constitutes Christianity. The circle is open for anyone who wishes to join.

The Christian Message is called the Gospel of Christ. The word "Gospel" means "Good News."

Life which is mere existence is not really life. It is indescribably drab. Pleasure, purpose and satisfaction must give it meaning. Amusements, diversions, hobbies, and vacations all serve to add pleasure. Sympathy, understanding and love make life more purposeful and satisfying as we find our place in relation to our fellowmen. Behind all this, however, there is the persistent consciousness, even in the most irreligious, that the answer to the ultimate significance of life must be in God.

Yet God is so far removed.

He is hidden behind some kind of mysterious veil that seems to whisper of His presence and then hide Him from our view. Since we live in a hard, material world, where the things that can be seen and felt and tasted are the things which seem obviously real, it is quite natural for most men to seek pleasure and satisfaction in these things rather than in the mystic pursuit of elusive spiritual values.

Yet, we instinctively feel that in these spiritual values must be the answer we seek. It is only because they have eluded us until we have become disillusioned about them that we have turned to the more obvious pleasures that are near at hand.

It is precisely at this point that we need the "Good News" of Jesus Christ. Jesus could never be limited to a few mystics with special religious insight. He appealed to all men. His sharpest critics were the religious specialists of His day, who objected to His friendship with people whose religious and moral reputation was questionable.

On the last day of a certain festival the priests followed the custom of pouring out a pitcher of water as a symbol of life. The mystic significance of the symbol was apparently appreciated only by a few, for on the same day Jesus cried out to the multitudes, "If any one thirst, let him come to me and drink. He who believes in me, as the scripture has said, 'Out of his heart shall flow rivers of living water'" (John 7:37-38). Jesus was limited by no static symbol. He offered life, like flowing water, in such a way that it was available to all. He has promised that His presence will continue as a living reality in this world. His Gospel is good news to everyone. He removes every obstacle so that all who come to Him may have abundant life.

The wonder of the Christian message is that the simple soul who can only with difficulty spell out the words of the Bible can be as pleasing to God as the clear-thinking scholar who practically knows the New Testament by heart; the weakling who is inherently unstable can be just as good a Christian as the iron-willed stalwart; the unimaginative plodder who goes to sleep reading either his newspaper or his Bible has the same opportunity to enjoy abundant life as the clear-eyed man of vision. Christ is no less available to the average individual who knows he will live his commonplace life in obscurity than he is to the famous Christian leader. On the other hand, the scholar, the stalwart, the man of vision, and the man of fame are at no disadvantage when they come to Him, and He does not scorn to use their gifts and abilities.

Christianity is absolutely unique in its appeal. On the one hand it offers no special advantages to anyone. On the other hand, it brings us the good news that there are no obstacles which can keep abundant life from any person.

The first obstacle that must fall is a mistaken idea about faith. We have a tendency to think of faith as a commendable human trait, like courage or trustworthiness. It is often looked upon as an attitude of heart or state of mind which some people have and others lack. Those who seem to have it are said to be more "religiously inclined" than others. When we define faith in this way, we immediately set up a division among human beings, so that some find it easy to be religious and others tend to consider themselves quite incapable of an active religious interest.

Jesus cuts right through this mistaken idea. He does not define faith as some inherent quality which men possess, by which they may unlock the door to spiritual truth. He does not say, "Faith is the way." In fact, He Himself is the way. He says, "I am the way, and the truth, and the life." "I am the light." "I am the bread of life." "I am the good shepherd." Etc.

When the good news of Christ is unfolded before us and we allow ourselves to see what it really means, we are captivated by it. When this happens, faith is born. Paul says, "So faith comes from what is heard, and what is heard comes by the preaching of Christ" (Romans 10:17). In other words, faith is the result of hearing the "Good News" of Christ. Hearing produces faith. No one can have faith until after he has heard the "Good News." The reason some people do not believe is that they have never allowed themselves the privilege of discovering what the "Good News" of Christ really is. They may know a few religious expressions and imagine that this is the whole Gospel. The doctrinal statement of Christianity, which is the verbal expression of the Living Truth, may have been mistaken for the Truth itself. As long as they say, "I see it," they will remain blind; when they say, "I am blind, open my blind eyes," they are in a position to begin to see what the Gospel really means.

Even in human relationships, it is the responsibility of each person who desires the confidence of others to make it possible for them to believe in him. Each person must, by his dependability and trustworthiness, earn the confidence of others. Likewise, Christ undertakes the full responsibility of inducing faith in Himself on the part of all who will permit Him to do so.

By believing in Christ, the New Testament means looking to Him even though we must confess that we cannot believe. A man once came to Jesus on behalf of his son who was possessed by an evil spirit. Jesus told him, "All things are possible to him who believes." The man then cried out, "I believe; help my unbelief!" His believing really consisted in coming to Jesus with his unbelief and Jesus heard his prayer (Mark 9:23-24). From this we understand that man's basic need is not more faith, but a willingness to face the full extent of his unbelief.

Abraham was a man of great faith. In fact, in the fourth chapter of Romans he is called "the father of all who believe." Yet it also says of Abraham, "In hope he believed against hope." This little phrase is filled with encouragement for the one who has trouble believing. It tells us that faith was no settled and placid thing even for Abraham. His faith consisted in depending on the promise of God when there was no hope of its being fulfilled. In those times he must have been conscious of great unbelief.

When I was converted, I was a complete unbeliever. Modern materialism had destroyed what faith I had in anything spiritual. Had I waited to build up some kind of faith, I fear I would never have been converted to Christ. Weary of the emptiness of life, however, I came to my pastor, the late Dr. Paul W. Rood, just to see if he could say anything that would help me. I told him of my bitterness toward those who had robbed me of my childhood faith. He showed me how to call to God even out of the darkness of my unbelief. The result was that I prayed a prayer something like this:

"Christ—if there is any Christ—you know the hunger of my heart. If sin is a reality I must be a sinner. Save me—if there is any salvation. I confess I cannot believe, but if there is any help for me, I need it."

I cannot say that anything startling happened to me at that moment. Faith did not suddenly dawn bright and clear. I was conscious of no emotional crisis. The only change was that I was now resigned to God, even though His very existence was an uncertainty to me. Unbelief was not the same active barrier that it had been. I cannot trace the steps whereby unbelief melted away, but I know that God did it.

Looking to Christ, just as we are, with our unbelief, confusion, and failure, is what the Bible means by faith. A consciousness of unbelief will be normal to a growing faith. This definition of faith may seem logically inconsistent to us, but so is human nature, and we can be eternally grateful that God has chosen to define faith in such a way that its first appeal is to human nature rather than to pure logic.

Illogical as it may seem, the great heroes of faith were often beset by unbelief, failure, and despair. Abraham had periods when his faith failed. Elijah is called "a man of like nature with ourselves." That is, he was a man who felt the same temptations to evil, despair, and unbelief that we do. David failed in time of temptation. Peter's courage forsook him on more than one occasion. They were men like us. They met God as they were, and God accepted them.

We have the good news to tell to all men that there is absolutely no barrier to Christ. That which appears to be the obstacle which keeps a certain person from Christ is in reality the very thing which will assure him an entrance into His presence. He who cannot believe, let him come with his unbelief. He who cannot understand may come with his confusion. The rebellious man may come if he will only bring his rebellion. The indifferent and the cold person may come with his indifference and coldness. He who is troubled with bitterness and deep feeling may bring his tangled emotions. He who has no feelings may come as he is. The moral failure may come with his failures knowing that Christ will forgive and continue to forgive as often as he fails.

The New Testament emphatically declares that Christ is immediately available to us just where we are:

> But the righteousness based on faith says, Do not say in your heart, "Who will ascend into heaven?" (that is, to bring Christ down) or "Who will descend into the abyss?" (that is, to bring Christ up from the dead). But what does it say? The word is near you, on your lips and in your heart (that is, the word of faith which we preach) . . . (Romans 10:6-8).

We are not to go anywhere to search for Christ. The word which we need in order to contact Him is right in our mouth and in our heart. There are no heights to achieve and no depths to plumb.

I used to preach a sermon on "Three Steps to Glory." I don't preach it any more because there are so many people who are too lame to climb the steps. For them, Christ may be found at the bottom of the first step. The New Testament tells of an invalid who was too weak to get into the Pool of Bethesda during the short interval while the waters retained their healing powers (John 5:2-9). Some of us are like him. We wait in vain beside innumerable pools which we believe would help us if we could only get to them. Jesus needs no pools. He, Himself, is all we need. He comes to us where we are, and the pools become superfluous.

This "Good News" is needed as much by believers as by unbelievers. Christ has many followers who are vainly trying to climb up to some spiritual heights or to descend to some spiritual depths in order to get closer to Him.

Because prayer is revitalized through fellowship with Christ, there is a tendency to look upon prayer as a way to Christ and to try vainly to pray more fervently in order to come closer to Him. The Bible speaks of Christ, and when Christ is near the Bible seems like a new Book. Therefore some torment themselves for not reading or studying it more faithfully in order to know Him better. Christ is the way to the Bible. The Spirit of Christ Himself must speak through the pages of the Scriptures before they can become meaningful. The period of daily personal devotions becomes a more blessed experience to those who know Christ intimately. Sometimes this tends to be looked upon as a way to Christ, and the responsibility to keep it only adds to the burden of a troubled conscience. The sheep do not come to the still waters to find the shepherd. It is the Shepherd Himself who leads them beside the still waters. These are not ways to bring us to Christ, or closer to Him. Christ is immediately available right where we are, as we are. He, in turn, becomes the way to these various means of worship. He leads us into those forms of personal devotion and worship which are most adapted to each one's spiritual needs. They do not lead us to Him.

Even the truth about Christ must not be substituted for Christ Himself, who is the Truth. Fellowship with Christ cannot be confined to any formulas or methods. Even the denial of formulas can in itself become a formula. The simple fact is that we must not be distracted either by formulas or lack of formulas from the person of Christ Himself. There is no place to climb up to get to Him; there are no depths to reach to get down to Him. He is right where we are.

> "We may not climb the heavenly steeps
> To bring the Lord Christ down;
> In vain we search the lowest deeps,
> For Him no depth can drown."

It has been very difficult for some of us to learn this lesson. One of the greatest spiritual experiences of my life resulted from the discovery that Christ did not require me to make any spiritual achievements before He would condescend to walk with me; that all the needs of my soul would be met when I had a broken and contrite spirit, when I repented and confessed my wrong-doing.

This experience helped me to see the futility of all self-effort. I discovered that repentance and a broken spirit were the only requirements for cleansing. However, having rejected all formulas for spiritual achievement, I made another mistake. I began to look upon repentance and a broken spirit as a way of life. I did not see that these had merely become another formula. They had become a way to Christ.

With great enthusiasm I preached release from captivity, but I was right back in bondage myself. The possession of information and principles that I thought others lacked brought me great satisfaction, but I knew no more of the liberty of Christ than they. Much as I feared to admit it, what I was teaching led to introspection and burdensome self-abasement. While others were trying to ascend to heaven to bring Christ down, I was descending to the depths to bring Him up.

When I was able to show others the benefits of my discovery, I was immensely pleased. I imagined myself to be an apostle of freedom, the restorer of New Testament truth to a Church in error. I expounded enthusiastically

and bored my friends endlessly at the slightest opportunity. When I met with opposition or indifference, I com-
forted myself with the thought that every ambassador of
truth must be prepared to be the target of persecution.

Christ spoke to me about my error through one of His
faithful servants who pointed out to me how proud I was
of my discovery. Finally I saw that I was just being
pleased with myself, that I loved to have men listen
to me, and that I pouted like a spoiled child when they refused. I had to recognize that I had no great discovery of
truth in which to boast. I could speak only of the same
Christ who had walked with God's children of all the
ages. If I wished to boast, I must be content, with all other
Christians, to boast in the Lord. It was a valuable experience, for it taught me how easy it is to substitute some
special application of the truth for Christ.

Christ, Himself, is immediately available to all who will
receive Him. This is good news, not only to the unconverted, but also to the weary Christian. Christ is the door;
all who will may enter. He is also the way; all who will
may walk thereon. There is no one so evil that he may
not come; no one so saintly that this should not still be
good news to him. There is no one so unbelieving and
rebellious that he may not bring his unbelief and rebellion
to Christ; there is no one so trusting and submissive that
he does not need to depend on the Shepherd to restore his
soul.

This is good news for all men. It is the only good news of which no one can say, "This is not for me." This is the "Good News" which is called "The Gospel of Christ."

CHAPTER TWO

The Teachings of Jesus

THE LOFTIEST ETHICAL PRINCIPLES ever to be revealed to man are found in the teachings of Jesus. No higher ideals have ever been conceived. Obviously a society guided by such principles would be far different from our world of today. Vice, corruption, misrepresentation, dishonesty, deceit, violence, war, and every other moral evil would be unknown. The resources and efforts which are now being expended to protect ourselves from our fellowmen could be diverted to useful channels. Technical skills and vast amounts of money would be released for research to make life more pleasant and beautiful. Love, peace, happiness, fair dealing, good will, and mutual concern would prevail.

It might seem, then, that being a Christian is largely a matter of learning the teachings of Jesus and of following them and seeking to persuade others to adopt them. Yet, although almost everyone agrees that the teachings of Jesus are quite wonderful, moral evil still persists in the world. His teachings are read, quoted, loved, and upheld; but there seems to be something that keeps people from adopting them as a way of life.

Jesus knew this would be the case, and He warned His disciples that they would be a minority which would often be misunderstood, hated and persecuted. The New Testament points out what it is that keeps people from applying His teachings. It declares that men are slaves to something which it calls "sin." As we shall see in the next chapter, "sin" is defined as something more than just immorality and unethical practices. It is a certain attitude toward God which men are powerless to change. Being a Christian, therefore, is more than just trying to follow the teachings of Jesus. His teachings are, of course, very important to the Christian, but Jesus means more to him than ethical principles. The New Testament brings us the "Good News" that, through Jesus Christ, we may be free from the dominion of sin.

CHAPTER THREE

The Dominion of Sin

A WOMAN CAME to our home by appointment one evening to discuss her problems. Reared in a thoroughly respectable home, she had attended church regularly during her youth. An unfortunate friendship had led to a way of life with which she herself was unhappy, and had severed her from her friends. Soon the moral pillars of her life began to crumble and she lost her self-respect. Her marriage failed through her own unfaithfulness, and every new turn of events seemed to bring temptations she could not overcome, until she had lost all incentive to resist. She was now adrift and subject to whatever influences were closest at hand. Her story was really quite shocking.

She knew how wrong she was, how out of touch with God and humanity, and how much of an enemy she was to herself. Her conscience was obviously troubling her and she was laboring under a sense of heavy guilt. Therefore, the statement she made when she was finished with her story was quite surprising. "People seem to think," she said, "that I am a terrible sinner. I can't see that I am such a bad person."

She wanted prayer for the improvement of her morals and her fortunes, and she felt quite distressed about the failure she had made of life, but she could not see herself as a sinner.

Her attitude was typical. There are few things more difficult to accept than Christianity's appraisal of all men as sinners. Even those who are obvious sinners find it difficult to see their sinfulness. There are others who seem to be nothing but personified goodness through and through. It seems even more difficult to look upon them as being sinners. What is the Biblical definition of sin? Just what does the New Testament mean when it says that "None is righteous, no, not one;" and that "all have sinned"?

Sin, as defined in the Bible, has to do with our relationship to God. In the most basic sense, it is possible to sin only against Him. "Against thee, thee only, have I sinned," said the Psalmist when he was repenting of his wrong-doing (Psa. 51:4). Actually no concept of sin is possible except in relationship to God. It is our ultimate responsibility to God that brings us face to face with sin.

Sin first appears in the third chapter of Genesis, the first book of the Bible, in the disobedience of Adam and Eve, who ate the forbidden fruit in the Garden of Eden. The act was sinful because it was an act of disobedience to the command of God, who had said, "You shall not eat of it." It was God's interest in the incident and His disapproval that made it sinful.

The fact that evil-doing results in social disapproval and unhappiness does not in itself make it sinful. On the other hand, the person who is law abiding and well-adjusted socially because he knows that evil-doing and crime do not pay is not thereby righteous. Those who disregard established moral laws are a menace and a problem to society, and must be dealt with accordingly. However, they are not necessarily more sinful than the more respectable citizens.

People are often troubled about the results of their misconduct and by what others think of them. They may have aspirations to do better, which may be more or less thwarted by temptations to do worse. Many times they will have great emotional disturbances as a result of their concern about their conduct. They may even pray to God to help them, and they may perform religious exercises and attend religious services because of the strength that religion promises. None of this is necessarily due to a sense of sinfulness. It may be the result of an intense desire to achieve a happy and well-adjusted life and to be accepted and approved by others.

Such distressing feelings, which result from the lack of social adjustment and approval, are often thought of as a sense of sinfulness. However, we must make it clear that the New Testament means something different from this when it speaks of confessing that we are sinners. A deep sense of sin will have a very sobering effect upon a person, but the New Testament never presents sin in such a way that recognizing it in ourselves should lead us to despair. Jesus never condemned anyone who recognized that he was a sinner. In fact, it was for just such people that He offered hope. Introspective examination and hopeless depression over our failings are the result of an unwillingness to recognize that we really are sinners. Once having accepted God's verdict that we are sinners, we can turn our attention to the good news that Christ offers to sinners.

On the other hand, there is just as much confusion about what the New Testament means by righteousness. People may be motivated by feelings of sympathy for others. They may derive great satisfaction from participation in philanthropic and community projects. They may have discovered the satisfying values of living orderly, moral, and useful lives. This is not what the New Testament means by righteousness. In this chapter we shall see how the New Testament defines sin. In the next chapter we shall see how it defines righteousness.

The origin of sin is described by Paul in Romans 1:21 as follows, "For although they knew God they did not honor him as God."

Man's sinfulness consists in *his refusal to honor God as God.* It is not necessarily a denial of the existence of God. It is not a rejection of the philosophical or religious concept of God. We are sinners even though we believe in God and worship Him. If God is God, His rightful place is at the very center of all existence, so that all of life revolves around Him. Our sinfulness consists in that God

is not given this place. Life for us does not rev[v]
God. It revolves around ourselves. Men have even gone
so far as to make gods of their own choosing in order to
make God conform to their own desires. Someone has cor-
rectly likened sin to anarchy. Crime is breaking the laws
of the State, but anarchy challenges the very right of the
State to make laws. Sin is more than breaking God's commandments. It challenges the very right of God to rule
as God.

It is not only the obviously selfish and wicked person
who rejects God as God so that life revolves around himself. The best people find satisfaction in their goodness
and success. Those who are the most altruistic are motivated by the fact that their altruism brings them personal
satisfaction. Even the person who seeks God does not do
so in order that He might be God to him, but that He
might provide certain benefits, either spiritual or material.
When Paul says, "No one seeks for God" (Roman 3:11),
he means that no one seeks God as God. If we seek God for
what He can do for us, we are really seeking a servant. We
are not really seeking God, for God can never be sought as
though He were a servant. The New Testament, therefore,
defines sin as something more than mere wrong-doing. It
is allowing life to revolve around ourselves instead of God.
The life of every one of us revolves around himself, and
God does not occupy the place of God to any of us. Therefore, we are all sinners. The power of sin over us is such
that it is impossible for us to change this situation.

The first temptation to sin, described in the third chapter of Genesis, has set the pattern for all sin. It was the temptation to question God, "Did God say?" and thus to refuse to honor God as God; and it was the temptation to become as God, "You will be like God," by setting up man's own judgment against the judgment of God (Genesis 3:1-5). When man once tasted the forbidden glory of being like God, it became impossible for him to return to the place of honoring God as God again. Henceforth life for man would continue to revolve around himself instead of God. In this way, the sin of the first man affected the entire human race.

This rejection of God as God, so that life revolves around ourselves instead of Him, is behind all moral and spiritual evil. One kind of moral evil is described in the first chapter of Romans where it is stated three times that "God gave them up" to all forms of degradation (Romans 1:24, 26, 28). Envy, murder, sexual immorality and perversion, gossip, insolence, ruthlessness, etc., are described as symptoms of man's refusal to allow God to be God to him. When men refused to honor God as God, they removed themselves from His dominion. He merely let them go. They became subject to overpowering passions which produced all forms of immorality. Sin, in other words, has become a power dominating man.

The second chapter of Romans describes another set of symptoms of man's rejection of God as God. These symptoms are found in the self-righteous person who passes judgment on others because of his possession of religious truth and knowledge of the will of God. He considers possession of God's law to be equal to obedience to the law. Yet, in judging others, he condemns himself, for he is unable to live up to the religion he embraces. Here again, sin is a dominating power, for it drives men to censoriousness and harsh judgment of others.

The final conclusion is a sweeping appraisal of all men as sinners, "None is righteous, no, not one" (Romans 3:10).

This description of sin as a power to which man has become a slave is emphasized throughout the New Testament. As Jesus said, "Everyone who commits sin is a slave to sin" (John 8:34). Sin has dominion, as a king over a kingdom. As we shall see in the next chapter, the "Good News" of Christ is the power to save people from the dominion of sin. It is not just good advice to tell them to mend their ways.

Sin rules by keeping self, instead of God, in the center of our lives. Therefore salvation from sin is to a certain extent salvation from ourselves. This is something which has been missed by some Christians who go about seeking ways to improve themselves when they really need to be saved from the self they are trying to improve.

The first step in saving men from sin must be something which will convince them of their sinfulness. Individuals must by some means be caused to agree willingly with God's verdict that they are sinners. Because sin is fundamentally a failure to honor God as God, and because sin exists only in relation to Him, its effect is to make men blind to their own sin. When men have once dethroned God and put self in His place, sin ceases to exist for them except as an abstract concept. Since God is no longer at the center of life, and men do not recognize His right to be there, they are no longer conscious of any rebellion against Him, and sin ceases to be sin for them. Therefore, the first step in reaching men must be to provide a means of convincing them that they are sinners.

The sinful deed of crucifying Jesus, for instance, was performed by men who should have been the best men of their times, and they made themselves believe they were serving God by doing it. In all their sinfulness, they refused to accept the fact that they were sinners. In the parable of the Pharisee and the Publican (Luke 18:9-14), it was the Pharisee who was under the dominion of sin. He was the one who could not see that he was a sinner. On the other hand, the Publican, who saw that he was a sinner, was released from his sin.

This inherent power of sin to blind us to our own sinfulness is summarized in Paul's appraisal of both the immoral person and the religious moralist.

The immoral person approves what he knows God disapproves: "Though they know God's decree that those who do such things deserve to die, they not only do them but approve those who practice them" (Romans 1:32).

To the moralist, Paul says: "But if you . . . rely upon the law and boast of your relation to God and know his will and approve what is excellent, because you are instructed in the law, and if you are sure that you are a guide to the blind, a light to those who are in darkness, a corrector of the foolish, a teacher of children, having in the law the embodiment of knowledge and truth—you then who teach others, will you not teach yourself?" (Romans 2:17-21).

In both of these cases men justify themselves. They approve of what they do, and are unable to recognize that anything is basically wrong. When God is no longer honored as God, sin ceases to be sin. Sin makes it impossible for us to see that we are subjects of a spiritual kingdom that refuses to honor God as God, that is completely at odds with God. Sin rules over us by making it impossible for us to see that we are enemies in active rebellion against God, and that, in this controversy, He is right and we are wrong.

Sin has the power to convince those who are its most obedient slaves that they themselves are free. When Jesus spoke to certain people of freedom, they replied, "We are descendents of Abraham, and have never been in bondage to anyone. How is it that you say, 'You will be made free'?" (John 8:33). They were full of resentment, ill will, and pride. Yet they considered themselves to be perfectly free.

God and man cannot be reconciled simply by God being gracious and loving enough to overlook our faults and forgive our sins. Release must be something more than ordinary forgiveness. It must be something which will redeem us from the power of sin so that God may again become God to us.

This has been accomplished by the act of redemption which God has performed through the death of Jesus Christ on the cross, and in the next chapter we shall see what the cross really means. There are no formulas or methods to break sin's power. Christ alone can do this. As we have now seen, sin has produced a changed perspective so that God is no longer honored as God, so that man seeks to justify himself and refuses to recognize that he is the sinner, worthy of death, for not giving God His rightful place. This is what is meant by the dominion of sin.

CHAPTER FOUR

What the Cross Really Means

A T THIS POINT I would like to add another person
to the little circle I am having particularly in mind
while I am writing. I was once speaking to an informal
group on the importance of the cross. When I had com-
pleted what I thought was a clear, concise exposition of the
cross, the meeting was opened for questions and discussion. The first question came from a young man who
asked, "What do you mean by the cross?"

I had just finished speaking in detail about the cross,
and here was a young person who did not even know what
I meant by the cross! What was far more disconcerting,
however, was the fact that I had so much difficulty trying
to explain to him just what the cross means. I could explain it quite fluently in theological terminology. Yet,
even while I was speaking I was aware that I was just
using words. I was quite at a loss to explain in expressions
which were meaningful to him what is really meant by
the cross. I began to question how much I myself really
knew about the cross. I hope that if this man will join
our little circle I can be more successful this time.

The cross of which Christians speak is the cross upon
which Jesus died. Most of us are quite familiar with the

41

historical details of Jesus' death on the cross, as described in the New Testament. Where we need help is in understanding the significance of this cross and why it is so important. Several terms which are used in the New Testament have the same meaning as "the cross." They are expressions dealing with the death of Christ. In the Epistle to the Romans, which deals in greater detail with the significance of the cross than any other part of the New Testament, the word "cross" does not even appear. This is quite interesting, for Paul, who wrote the Epistle to the Romans, uses the term quite frequently in several other epistles. Whatever may be the reason, we should remember that such expressions as "the cross," "the blood," etc. refer to the death of Jesus and to what His death may mean to us.

"The cross" is a symbolic expression, but we are not interested in the cross just as a symbol. Christ's death on the cross is the means whereby God does certain momentous things for human beings. When we speak of the cross, therefore, we are referring to everything the dying of Jesus on the cross signifies.

Before we discuss the significance of the cross itself there are two principles, clearly emphasized by the Apostle Paul, which we should have in mind. They are:

(1) *The cross is central.*

The cross is central in all the preaching and teaching of Paul. Everything that he says revolves around the cross and the death of Jesus. The following statements will serve to illustrate this fact:

> *For I decided to know nothing among you except Jesus Christ and him crucified (I Corinthians 2:2).*
> *But far be it from me to glory except in the cross of our Lord Jesus Christ (Galatians 6:14).*
> *For Christ did not send me to baptise but to preach the Gospel, and not with eloquent wisdom, lest the cross of Christ be emptied of its power (ICorinthians 1:17).*

Later we shall have occasion to refer again to the centrality of the cross. In interpreting what Paul means by certain statements on which there is a difference of opinion, we shall consistently interpret them in conformity with his emphasis on the importance of the cross.

(2) *The cross is foolishness.*

Paul often warns us that, from the standpoint of human logic, the cross is utter folly. The following statements will illustrate:

> *For the word of the cross is folly to those who are perishing, but to us who are being saved it is the power of God (I Corinthians 1:18).*
> *. . . it pleased God through the folly of what we preach to save those who believe (I Corinthians 1:21).*

We must remember that we normally think of everything in relation to ourselves. The message of the cross is from another perspective, which may seem quite illogical to us. Therefore we must give consideration to every new propositions about the cross, no matter how illogical or

offensive it may seem. We shall discover that the propositions about the cross fit together in a different kind of logic
and that they all come out right in the end.

As we begin to consider the real meaning of the cross,
therefore, let us tuck away in the back of our minds these
two principles: (1) The cross is central in everything
Paul says; (2) Many propositions related to the cross will
probably appear quite foolish and offensive from the
human standpoint. We shall have occasion to refer to
these two principles more than once, and we shall discover
that they are immeasurably helpful in clarifying statements which would otherwise be quite confusing.

Among all the various things that the dying of Jesus
on the cross means, we shall confine ourselves to four,
which have the most practical significance to us:

1. *By dying on the cross, Jesus settled the question of
who is wrong in the controversy between God and man.*

In the last chapter we saw how the dominion of sin
over men makes it impossible for us to recognize that we
are really sinners. From our viewpoint, we constantly
seek to justify ourselves. From God's viewpoint, however,
we are sinners because we refuse to honor God as God.
This is the real controversy between God and man.

When God took the form of man and lived here on
earth personified in Jesus, this controversy was brought
to a head. The inevitable result was the cross. When we
look at the historical events leading to the crucifixion of
Jesus, there can be no question about who is at fault.

Jesus lived among us. We saw Him as a man who went about doing nothing but good, condemning nothing but evil, being a blessing wherever He went. He did absolutely nothing to deserve crucifixion. We were required to recognize that His crucifiers were the sinners.

That is why it was so important that He be crucified in Jerusalem. The men who instigated the crucifixion had more opportunity then anyone else to know the will and purpose of God. They had a literature and a tradition which included the great prophets of God for centuries preceding. If we look upon them as the worst of all men, we forget that they have been viewed by all history side by side with Jesus. Beside Him any of us would have appeared black. There is no way that we can consistently see ourselves any better than they. Jerusalem was the brightest spot in a dark world, and it was Jerusalem that crucified Christ. In the crucifixion of Christ, the controversy between God and man is pinpointed so clearly that we cannot remain blind to who is at fault. It took the cross to settle this question with complete finality. On the cross Jesus settled for all time the fact that man is a sinner in rebelling against God.

2. *The death of Jesus on the cross was God's supreme gesture of reconciliation.*

> **All this is from God, who through Christ reconciled us to himself and gave us the ministry of reconciliation; that is, God was in Christ reconciling the world to himself, not counting their trespasses against them, and entrusting to us the message of reconciliation. So**

we are ambassadors for Christ, God making his appeal through us. We beseech you on behalf of Christ, be reconciled to God (II Corinthians 5:18-20).

When men hung Jesus on the cross, He made no counter-attack. "Like a sheep that before its shearers is dumb, so he opened not his mouth" (Isaiah 53:7). During those agonizing hours on the cross no vindictive word escaped His lips. God's attitude toward us was expressed in the prayer offered by His Son, "Father, forgive them, for they know not what they do."

The cross was God's expression that He desires nothing but reconciliation with man. There is nothing but kindness and love on God's part.

3. *Christ died on the cross for our sins.*

The New Testament expresses this in many places, such as:

Christ died for our sins (I Corinthians 15:3).
. . . while we were yet sinners Christ died for us (Romans 5:8).
. . . our Lord Jesus Christ, who died for us . . . . (I Thessalonians 5:9-10).
He himself bore our sins in his body on the tree (I Peter 2:24).

The full meaning of all this will of necessity transcend human understanding, and theology has many different ways of expressing as much as we are able to comprehend, but this much is clear from the New Testament: When Christ died on the cross, God through Christ assumed all the responsibility for our rebellion against Him and all the evil that resulted from it. Christ took *our* sins on Him-

self and died for them. This means that God therefore
holds no charge whatsoever against us. In Colossians 2:14,
Paul states that He "canceled the bond which stood against
us with its legal demands; this he set aside, nailing it to the
cross." Thus, by sending His Son to die on the cross for
us, God set aside the power of sin to condemn us. God condemned sin so we may be free from condemnation. Farther
on, in Romans 8:3, Paul uses a similar expression. He says
that when God sent His Son, Jesus Christ, to earth, "He
condemned sin in the flesh." For God to condemn sin was,
of course, no mere mechanical transaction. It was done at
great sacrifice to Himself, for it cost Him His own Son.
The extent of the cost to God indicates how seriously He
considers sin.

The law of God condemns the sinner. It says, "The
soul that sins shall die" (Ezekiel 18:4). The only response the sinner can make is to seek to justify himself
and to prove that he is not a sinner, or perhaps to say that
God is not really as serious about sin as He appears. Therefore, the law against sin which condemns the sinner can
never settle the controversy between God and man.

At the cross, however, God did just the opposite. Instead of condemning sinners, he condemned their sin.
This means that He destroyed the power of sin to condemn us. When Christ assumed the responsibility for all
our sins and died for them, He thereby set us free from
condemnation. When men condemned the sinless Christ to
a sinner's death, God did not retaliate by condemning the

men who did it. In the Person of Christ, He took their sin upon Himself when Christ died for sin. Therefore men may be free from the condemnation which results from sinning against God. "For our sake he made him to be sin who knew no sin, so that in him we might become the righteousness of God" (II Corinthians 5:21). He destroyed sin's power to condemn the sinner. Therefore, the sinner is free.

That God condemned sin also means that He destroyed the power of sin to blind us to our own sinfulness. As we saw in the preceding chapter, sin rules over us by causing life to revolve around ourselves. This is being constantly confirmed in practical living. Each one of us is most satisfying to himself. We vote for the political candidate whom we think will most benefit us personally. "The life that you save may be your own" is an effective safety slogan because each person instinctively values his own life above that of anyone else. Every moral evil in the world; every act of violence; every misunderstanding, between husband and wife, or beween nations, results from the fact that the life of each one revolves around himself.

This fact makes it impossible to honor God as God for, if God is to be God, life must revolve around Him. It seems so natural for life to revolve around ourselves, that men cannot accept this as sinful. Through the death of Christ, however, God condemned sin by destroying its power to keep us from seeing our sinfulness; so that we can accept the fact that we really are sinners. On the cross He revealed sin for what it is.

He revealed sin's intrigue. He revealed to us how completely we have rejected God, how Jesus could be condemned as a blasphemer, how dignified religious leaders could stoop to ridicule Him for His helplessness on the cross. He revealed to us how we could look upon Him as being a criminal, deserving the cross as a punishment from God; how we considered ourselves to be right and Him to be wrong.

He revealed sin's power to destroy. He showed us the sweat and the tears and the blood. He unmasked it before us in such a way that we could see that the sinfulness was all on our side.

God did not condemn sin just by an edict from heaven, which we might say we cannot understand or recognize or believe. He condemned sin right on this earth, where it could become a matter of human record. The cross leaves us no opportunity to say that sin doesn't matter. All the morbid effects of man's rebellion against God stand out in clear perspective at the cross. In a body of flesh, in the likeness of ourselves, God revealed sin for what it really is.

At the cross each one of us as an individual must see himself. Every repulsive detail is a reflection of the nature of my sin. I, not God, am responsible for the cross, for it is my sinfulness that made the cross necessary in the purpose of God. All its bloody repugnance is my repugnance. If the horrible event of the crucifixion of Jesus is the result of my sinfulness, how terrible must that sinfulness be. At the cross my sin was uncloaked so that I can see it for what it really is.

Sin is personified in the New Testament. It is likened to a king who is in constant rebellion against God. King Sin has led all his subjects into rebellion and he has succeeded in causing them to think of themselves as gods, so that each one looks upon life from the perspective of himself, as though he were at the very center of life. All the conflict and disorder among men is caused by the fact that each one looks upon life from a different viewpoint and no one places God at the center of life.

In order to put down this rebellion, God may either condemn all these wayward subjects of King Sin; or He may condemn King Sin himself and reveal him to be the rebel that he is, and then be merciful to all those subjects who will confess their waywardness and again recognize His right to rule over them.

God took the latter course through the dying of Jesus on the cross. He did not condemn the rebelling subjects. He delivered up His Son to King Sin. The result revealed the true nature of both God and King Sin. King Sin was condemned as a rebel and God offered his subjects mercy. Those who continue under the rule of King Sin remain under condemnation, no matter how good their ethics or morals may be, for they live unto themselves and refuse to honor God as God. Those who accept God's offer of mercy, however, are no longer under condemnation, and since King Sin has now been condemned, he loses his authority over them.

4. *The cross, therefore, is an invitation from God to come and be reconciled to Him.*

God made it clear that there is no barrier to Himself. He has assured us that He will hold no man's sin against him. He, Himself, has assumed the responsibility for it.

One thing, however, remains to be done. This is something that man alone can do. God cannot do it for him. In the Person of Christ, God came down to us, and we saw His glory. He hung on a cross, yet even the undignified death of the cross only magnified His glory, for it revealed God to be only love personified. There was no vindictiveness, only love. He *bore* our sins and returned only love. The power of sin both to condemn us and to blind us to our own sinfulness is broken when we are brought face to face with the cross, so that we are enabled to see that it is we who are sinners in rebelling against such a God. God therefore calls upon us to confess it and to agree with Him in His appraisal of us as sinners. This is what the New Testament means by repentance. Repentance means to agree with God against ourselves. Without this, nothing that happened on the cross can be effective, for man still continues to justify his rebellion against God. The cross brings us to repentance by revealing us to be sinners.

Repentance is merely recognizing that it is sin to let life revolve around ourselves instead of God, thereby confessing that we are sinners in that we do not honor God as God. Repentance is not shifting our life center from ourselves to God. This is impossible even for the most repentant person to do, for life still revolves around self. There is no salvation in repentance itself. It is the cross that brings us to repentance, but even the cross does not give us the power to save ourselves. It invites us to trust entirely in Christ to save us.

The moment a person repents of the sinfulness of not honoring God as God, and confesses it to be sin, he ceases to be an enemy of God. God and he are now in agreement, and he is at peace with God. This is possible because, though he is still a sinner, God holds no charge against him, for Christ on the cross assumed the responsibility for his sin. At that moment, therefore, God declares him to be righteous.

The term in the New Testament to describe this declaration by God that we are righteous is "justification." Wherever this term is found in the New Testament it means that God has declared us to be righteous. This righteousness is known as the righteousness of faith. It is based on the faith which is induced when we come face to face with the cross and see what sinners we are in not honoring God as God, and when we see that Christ died for our sins on the cross and that God now holds no charge against us. When we see what God has done for us, faith is born.

Jesus also promised that we would have the help of the Spirit of God, whom He called "the Counselor" or "the Comforter," to convince us of these spiritual realities. "And when he comes," Jesus said, "he will convince the world of sin and of righteousness and of judgment" (John 16:8). He helps us to see our own sinfulness, to understand what God's righteousness really is, and to comprehend other spiritual things. In this way He also makes faith possible.

The righteousness of God by faith is not dependent on personal conduct, obedience to God's legal requirements, or a change in nature. It is simply a declaration of God that we are righteous when we agree with God's verdict that we are sinners in rebelling against Him. We have now ceased being enemies of God. "Therefore, since we are justified by faith, we have peace with God through our Lord Jesus Christ" (Romans 5:1). We do not work to become righteous or to improve ourselves in God's sight. As Paul says, "And to one who does not work but trusts Him who justifies the ungodly, his faith is reckoned as righteousness" (Romans 4:5).

Thus we are brought face to face with the great paradox of the cross; that we are made righteous when we see ourselves to be sinners. We shall see in the following chapters that this paradox continues as an ever unfolding mystery throughout the entire Christian life, and that sin loses all its power by the application to Christian living of what Christ has done on the cross.

We may now summarize the real meaning of the cross as follows: (1) In the crucifixion of Jesus, the controversy between God and man was brought to a head so it is clear, even to us, that we are sinners in not honoring God as God, and in permitting life to revolve around ourselves instead of Him. (2) On the other hand, the cross was God's supreme gesture of reconciliation, by which He shows, through Christ, that He is completely free from vindictiveness and that He desires only reconciliation. (3) Through the cross God wiped out every charge which was based on the requirements of the law, because Christ died for our sins. (4) Having done all this, He invites us to recognize that we are sinners in rebellion against Him as God, and to turn against our own sin and accept His complete pardon. He will hold our sins against us no longer. We are actually redeemed from the dominion of sin through the cross. The price of our redemption or ransom is the blood of Christ (I Peter 1:18-19). Sin loses its power to blind us to the sinfulness of our rebellion against God so that we may come repentant, seeking His pardon. Sin also loses its power to condemn us, for God now holds nothing against us. This is what the cross really means.

CHAPTER FIVE

Applying the Cross to Christian Living

IN NORMAL CHRISTIAN EXPERIENCE, the cross will continue to be effective throughout all of our lives. This means that we must continue to accept God's verdict that we are still sinners, and that we must continue to trust in God's pardon, which we received when we first became believers.

This certainly was Paul's experience. After he had been a Christian for many years, he still considered himself to be the foremost of sinners (I Timothy 1:15). We must also remember that it was as a Christian that he said, "But far be it from me to glory except in the cross of our Lord Jesus Christ" (Galatians 6:14). The cross, with its promise of pardon, was still at the very heart of his own experience. Sometimes Christians begin to think that after years of Christian living they should have improved to some extent so they are not quite as much in need of God's pardon for their sinfulness. This sense of self-sufficiency directs their attention from the cross. They are not quite as dependent on what Christ did on the cross for them. Christian experience then begins to fade.

The word "grace" appears often on the pages of the New Testament. Grace is what God has done and is doing for us out of pure mercy, because we are undeserving and have nothing with which to repay Him. Grace is God's way of giving His blessings as a free gift, expecting nothing in return, and asking only that we receive them. Grace is behind all that God has done for us and in us, but it refers particularly to His redemptive work, which is based on what Christ did on the cross. "They are justified," Paul says, "by his grace as a gift, through the redemption which is in Christ Jesus" (Romans 3:24).

Grace really springs out of the fact that God is Creator and we are His creatures. The source of all life is in the Creator. He must give and His creatures must receive. There can be no other relationship. Our recognition of God as God, requires that we be willing to accept it. We must be willing to receive what God offers. The fact that He offers righteousness implies that we must recognize our sinfulness, for only sinners can receive righteousness as a gift. As the sun gives its light to the earth, expecting nothing in return except what may be a reflection of its own light, just so, the Creator gives to His creatures, expecting nothing in return except what may be a reflection of what He, Himself, is doing.

Paul, in I Corinthians 15:10, declares that this kind of relationship exists between God and him. First he says, "By the grace of God I am what I am." Then he refers to what he has done, "His grace toward me was not in vain.

On the contrary, I worked harder than any of them." Finally, he says that what was done was only God in His grace working in him, "It was not I, but the grace of God which is with me."

Man's sinfulness in not honoring God as God, persists in those who are devoutly religious. Here it often takes the form of assuming some credit for what seems to be a superior devotion. Perhaps the person who is serving God faithfully feels that he deserves a little more consideration than others, or the person who is very devout feels that he is not quite as much a sinner as certain other Christians. This attitude nullifies the grace relationship, for it assumes that man, to some extent, can be made more acceptable to God by responding to God's commandments in a better way than someone else. Paul condemns it in no uncertain terms. "I do not nullify the grace of God," he says, "for if justification were through the law, then Christ died to no purpose" (Galatians 2:21). "Now to one who works," he also says, "his wages are not reckoned as a gift but as his due. And to one who does not work but trusts him who justifies the ungodly, his faith is reckoned as righteousness" (Roman 4:4-5).

If, for the sake of respectability, reputation or personal satisfaction, we try to be something more than sinners, we presume to disagree with God, for He has said that we are sinners. We have then usurped the place of God, and He is not really God to us. This makes the Christian life laborious. At the cross, it is not what *we do*. It is what

Christ has done. It must always be sufficient for us that Christ died on the cross for our sins.

Romans 6:1-14 is a passage which is basic to Christian living. It is unfortunate that there is so much confusion about its application. However, if we remember that the cross is also basic to Christian living, and if we interpret this passage in the light of the cross, it becomes at once both practical and applicable.

This passage begins as follows: "What shall we say then? Are we to continue in sin that grace may abound? By no means! How can we who died to sin still live in it?"

In what sense has the Christian died to sin? Paul cannot be referring to this as an ideal or achievement in Christian living, for he speaks of it in the past tense, as something that has already happened. It is the first time in the Epistle to the Romans that he uses the idea of Christians having died to sin. Yet he does not introduce it as being something new.

We have no right to assume that Paul throws unrelated propositions into his development of thought, with meanings that are not dependent on what has preceded, without any indication that something new is being considered, and with no explanation of what they mean, so that we are left to speculate on their proper interpretation. If this were the case, it would be folly to attempt to follow any Biblical analysis. By dying to sin, Paul can mean only one thing: He is looking back in retrospect upon what he has already said. It is a summary of his development of thought up to this point.

It may well be true, as has been suggested by some, that the expression of "dying to" something was a common one in Paul's time, and would be understood by those to whom he was writing. However, it would still be necessary for him to relate this expression to Christian teaching. Having discussed the significance of Christ's death for sinners, Paul turns to those who have accepted the benefits of His death, and, using this expression to describe what has happened from their viewpoint, he says in effect, "You have died to sin."

Paul has already established that all men are sinners because no one honors God as God, and that none can become righteous by trying to do better. Those who have repented of their sin and who are trusting in God's grace in redeeming man through Christ's death, are declared righteous. They recognize that they are sinners, and sin cannot any longer condemn them, for Christ died for them. After Paul has discussed all of this, he says, "You have died to sin." Dying to sin, therefore, does not mean to stop being sinners. It does not mean that all impulses to sin are dead in the Christian so he is no longer subject to temptation to sin. It simply means to recognize that we are sinners, repent of it, and accept God's pardon so that sin can condemn us no more. Certainly nothing else could have been in the mind of Paul, for he never discusses

anything else that could possibly apply to dying to sin in
any other way. Dying to sin, dying to self, crucifying self,
being crucified with Christ, dying to the world, and similar
expressions may be said, for our purposes at least, to mean
very much the same thing. They do not refer to a higher
kind of Christian living. They refer to an attitude of repentance and brokenness, and an acceptance of God's pardon for sin through what Christ has done on the cross.

The statements that follow immediately (Romans
6:3-5) further clarify that this is what Paul means by
saying that we have died to sin. Paul goes on to say that
we have been united with Christ in a death and resurrection like His. What was His death like? We have the answer in Romans 6:10, "The death he died he died to sin."
His dying to sin did not mean that He stopped being a sinner for He was not a sinner even before His death. Dying
to sin had nothing to do with His personal character. Before His death, however, sin had the power to condemn
Him to die on the cross. The important thing is that when
He died, sin lost its power to condemn Him. That we have
been united with Him in a death like His, therefore, means
that sin has lost its power to condemn us. Dying to sin for
us simply means that we repent and accept God's pardon,
for this is the way of release, for us, from sin's condemnation. It does not refer to the question of whether we are or
are not sinners. It does not mean that we have become
free from temptation and the sense of our own sinfulness.

This is all a part of the unique logic of the cross, to which we have already referred, which seems so foolish to human reason. We die to sin by recognizing that we are sinners. Sinners are declared righteous by faith. Everything seems just the opposite of what it should be, for we are seeing things from God's viewpoint, in which we are no longer central.

During a certain period of my life I became greatly interested in a critical analysis of Christendom as it operates today. I discovered great flaws and weaknesses in every branch of Christianity. All of this distressed me intensely and I became quite unhappy. I interpreted my sadness as a great concern for God's glory.

Then, during a Gospel service, the Spirit of God called my attention to a deep-seated resentment I had toward a certain fellow pastor who had been quite successful. I had felt critical toward him before, but I had always justified my attitude. Now, however, I saw myself as the sinner. The recognition of my sinfulness confirmed God's verdict that I was a sinner and that there was pardon for me. The result was a great sense of peace because I was in complete agreement with God's appraisal of me, and Christ brought me His blessing and release.

This minister toward whom I had felt so resentful was present at at informal meeting which was held a few days later. His presence afforded me an opportunity to witness how the Lord, in His redemptive work, had set me free from my resentment. However, I cringed at the very idea

of giving such a testimony. Again, I was forced to recognize that my embarrassment was due to a strong pride
which made me unwilling to be known for what I really
was. This again was sin, which only further confirmed
God's appraisal of me as a sinner. "Thou art surely right, O
God," I prayed, "in judging me to be a sinner." The moment I accepted God's verdict, Christ brought me new release. There was no longer any point in trying to hide the
fact that I was a sinner, and it was a joy to witness of
God's work in my heart.

I didn't realize until several weeks later that my critical
attitude toward the weaknesses of the Church had melted
away. It had all been tied up with my unconscious resentment.

This is God's precise way of destroying the power
of sin. It allows us no opportunity to look lightly on sin
or to excuse it. The very fact that we look upon it as sin
causes us to oppose it. On the other hand, it does not leave
us in despair, for, in the same act of redemption in which
God revealed us to be sinners, He also offered us pardon.
However, when we try to prove that we have the power
to overcome sin, we are not dependent on the cross in this
particular instance, and we begin to boast in something
else than the cross. We may not recognize it in ourselves,
but by proving that we can overcome sin, we are putting
self again in the center of our lives. We say in effect, "I
am able to do better. I am not as bad as God says I am."

The cross captures us by bringing us to repentance so we have no greater desire than to turn from our sin. When sin appears in our life, it only proves God to be right in His appraisal of us as sinners, and this only leads to greater repentance. In either case, we can claim nothing but the grace of God. From our viewpoint, this is dying to sin. It is God's way of breaking the power of sin by leaving us nothing in which to boast except in Christ and His cross.

This brings us right back to the place where we began in the first chapter: Christ will meet us right where we are. He does not require us to be improved in some way before He can bless us. He wants us merely to recognize ourselves for what we are, where we are, and leave to Him the matter of making us what He wants us to be. If, indeed, salvation is to be by means of redemption, it must be accomplished in this way.

Romans 6:1-2 may, therefore, be paraphrased this way: "What shall we say then? Shall we continue to live in rebellion against God so that He may continue to be gracious to us in forgiving our sinfulness? By no means! We have died to sin by the very act of accepting God's verdict that we are sinners and by repenting of our sin. By so doing, we have agreed with God about our sin. Having done this, we obviously cannot continue to live in rebellion against God. To do so would be to take an attitude exactly opposite to what we took when we became Christians."

Let us now look at Romans 6:11: "So you also must consider yourselves dead to sin and alive to God in Christ Jesus."

Some have tried, with varying success, to apply this as though it meant to turn a deaf ear to the temptation to sin, to affirm that we *will* not respond to the call of sin. Considering ourselves dead to sin, however, can only mean to continue to do what we did when we first died to sin. In the light of the cross, therefore, it means to continue to consider ourselves to be sinners who have agreed with God about our sin, who are free from the condemnation of sin and who trust only in God's mercy through what Christ has done. Evidences of sin in our lives then only confirm God's verdict that we are sinners and bring us to repentance. By this means even the sin within us is turned against itself by leading us continually to repentance.

A Christian leader was witnessing to God's redemptive work in his life. He told how he had been very zealous for what he had thought was a good cause. In his zeal he had become tense and restless and had made things a bit difficult in his home. He told of how God had shown him that he was working in his own strength for his own glory. In his zeal he had thought of himself as a self-sacrificing person. The Lord had broken him and shown him that he was really just a sinner, who needed the grace of God. As a result, Christ had brought a new harmony to his home.

When he had finished, a lady rose to her feet and said, "If this man can afford to be a sinner, surely I can afford to recognize that I am a sinner. God has just shown me how my relationships with others are being disrupted by things in my own life that I have been blaming on them. I have just seen that I am the sinner."

These people were witnessing about how God had helped them to consider themselves dead to sin by helping them to accept the fact that they were sinners so that they might repent of their sins and confess their dependence on God's pardon.

Contrary to what some might think, it does not have a destructive or depressing effect to accept ourselves as sinners, for once having done so, we find ourselves in perfect agreement with God about ourselves. God is vindicated in His appraisal of us, and since this can happen only at the cross, we are right at the place where sin is condemned and we are set free.

However, it can be quite distressing to those who have not yet repented of sin, for such people are still struggling with the humiliation and embarrassment of setting themselves forth as being sinners. It is doubly difficult for them if they enjoy some reputation for piety and religious fervor. Sometimes the distress is so great that they cannot bear to continue to let the light shine upon them. Others may be tempted to look for some sin to confess so that they may have the satisfaction of having a share in being sinful. This will never do, however. It is just as sinful to glory in our sinfulness as it is to glory in our righteousness.

Some have continued for months and even years in a broken and contrite spirit, quietly accepting God's verdict of their sinfulness and their need of His pardon, but being conscious of no particular evidence of their sinfulness. Then suddenly something has awakened them to the full extent of their sin and they have been completely overwhelmed. When this has happened, the cross has become even more meaningful to them. In either case, God was with them. We must not seek to try to make ourselves feel either more sinful or more righteous. The important thing is not how sinful we feel, but that we accept God's verdict that we are sinners. We are saved by Christ, not by the degree of our feeling of sinfulness. Introspection is an enemy of grace, and we are much safer if we keep our attention on Christ and see ourselves only in relation to Him. It is He, Himself, who is the way.

Sin is to the Christian life what dirt is to a house. To deal with sin is as normal as for a housewife to dust or sweep. Dirt is not scandalous unless we parade it, allow it to accumulate, or sweep it under the rug. The same is true of sin. We must expect to deal with it continually through continual repentance.

When we consider ourselves dead to sin, we also consider ourselves alive to God (Romans 6:11). Having recognized our sinfulness, we also accept God's pardon so that we are free from condemnation. When we agree with God, we take sides with Him against our sin; He then becomes our Master. As Paul points out in the verses that follow (vs. 12-13), we should not let sin reign in our mortal bodies; we should not yield our bodies as instruments of sin, but to God, as instruments of righteousness. Sin is never acceptable to the Christian mind. Our bodies should never be yielded to evil. We should never consent to sin. We shall continue to find sin within us, but it ought never be with our consent. Having taken sides against our sinfulness, we should be prepared to recognize every sign of sin as further evidence of our need of the cross.

The New Testament makes no clear-cut distinction between a Christian's faith and the effect of his faith on the way he lives. Those who deliberately live contrary to Christian morals are said to "live as enemies of the cross of Christ" (Philippians 3:18-19). In other words, the cross is more than a symbol of certain religious beliefs. It affects our attitude toward life. An unrepentant spirit is enmity to the cross. An unrepentant person is actually blind to his sin. He has not allowed the cross to reveal to him what sin really is. His attitude is enmity to the cross no matter what his religious profession may be.

The real emphasis in the sixth chapter of Romans is not death but life. Many people make the mistake of trying to find some profound principle of dying to sin in this chapter, and of some means of applying it to Christian experience. In so doing, they miss the point.

The Christian has already died to sin. Paul has discussed all that in the third, fourth, and fifth chapters. Now, he turns to the other side of the picture. Dying to sin also means coming alive to God. The reason we should consider ourselves dead to sin is that we may be alive to God.

If we read this chapter without allowing our minds to get detained at the first mention of death, we see that the entire chapter is a transition from death to life. Every proposition begins with death and ends with life.

This, however, is not to be considered an advancement in Christian experience. It is merely a further development of the same truth. The same repentance and faith which makes us dead to sin also makes us alive to God. We do not first turn from sin and then turn to God. We turn from sin to God in one act. This was true in our first experience of meeting Christ in repentance and faith. No person will ever be more dead to sin than he is at the moment when he comes to Christ in repentance and receives Him as his Saviour. After this, it is by continual repentance that he considers himself to be dead to sin. By this same continual repentance, he considers himself to be alive to God.

Like the disciples who sought the body of Jesus in the tomb, not knowing that He was risen, we are sometimes guilty of seeking the living among the dead. Let us not look for tombstones in the sixth chapter of Romans, for every tomb has been opened. This is no morbid discourse on more effective ways of dying. It offers no grounds for speculation on what it means to die. Paul has already established that the cross of Christ is the way of dying.

At the cross we die to sin by recognizing our own sinfulness and accepting God's pardon. He now goes on to say that this very same way of dying to sin is the way of becoming alive to God, so that our life is lived unto Him.

This brings us to Romans 6:14, the climax of the entire passage, "For sin will have no dominion over you, since you are not under law but under grace."

This statement had been a great stumbling block to a certain Christian woman. She had discovered within herself what seemed to be many evidences of the dominion of sin. At times she was resentful. She sometimes lost her temper and said things she knew a Christian should not say. Though she had prayed much and sought God's help, she could not overcome these sins. This passage promised that sin would not have dominion over her, and yet she seemed obviously to be a slave to sin. Was there something wrong with her faith?

When she saw what this passage really meant in the light of the cross, she blossomed like a flower in the spring sunshine. She simply had to recognize that every resentment and every outburst of temper must be accepted as confirmation of God's verdict and she really was a sinner. "Why," she said, "I really am a sinner! My very sin has proven God to be right!" Once having accepted the fact that she was a sinner, she had no further need to justify her resentment and temper. Therefore, she found no difficulty in repenting and asking her friends for forgiveness whenever it was necessary. After a time the resentiments began to melt away and the outbursts of temper grew less frequent. The very thing which seemed to her to be evidence that she was under the dominion of sin was what God wished to use to demonstrate that she was free from sin by bringing her to repentance. Her release from the dominion of sin did not consist in that her disposition changed but in that she could accept the fact that she was a sinner whose only hope lay in God's pardoning grace. Her change in disposition was merely the fruit which eventually resulted from brokenness and repentance.

"For sin will have no dominion over you, *since you are not under law but under grace.*" If we were under law we would be under obligation to overcome temptation and become righteous by our good deeds. Furthermore, we would be under a constant sense of guilt, and we would be torn between despair at our failures and the frustration of trying to appear in as good a light as possible. Being under grace, however, we can afford to accept the fact that we are sinners. In fact we must be sinners in order to obtain grace. Because we are under grace, sin has no power to condemn us. Just as we discovered previously (Chapter Three) that the dominion of sin is the power of sin to keep us from seeing our sinfulness and need of God's pardon, we now discover that when the dominion of sin is broken we *do* see our sinfulness and accept God's pardon. This can only take place when we are not under law but under grace. Law condemns us for being sinners and drives us to seek to justify ourselves. Grace pardons our sin and invites us to accept the full extent of our sinfulness. This is the New Testament way of destroying the power of sin in Christian experience.

From the viewpoint of human reason, this seems to be utter folly. We come out just the opposite from where we would expect. We would like to come out in such a way that we could see ourselves as upright, respectable, successful Christians. However, the cross requires us to look at ourselves from God's viewpoint. From His viewpoint we are sinners, and any other conclusion than this is in opposition to Him. The cross does not make us sinners. It merely reveals our sin and invites us to confess it. At the cross we are never permitted any achievements in which to boast, neither are we left in despair over sin. The very recognition of our sinfulness makes it possible for Christ to break the power of sin and we become alive to God. Yet we are never permitted to see ourselves as more than sinners. Thus we must glory only in the cross.

> "Bane and blessing, pain and pleasure,
> By the cross are sanctified;
> Peace is there that knows no measure,
> Joys that through all time abide."

This Way may seem unpopular and offensive. However, we must realize that Paul meant what he said when he proclaimed the cross to be folly from the viewpoint of human reason. Jesus warned us, "Blessed is he who takes no offense at me" (Luke 7:23). When Paul defends this way, he recognizes that it will be a stumbling-block. He rejects other ways which might seem more reasonable, for, he says, "in that case the stumbling-block of the cross has been removed" (Galatians 5:11). There would be nothing offensive about a way that would permit us to see ourselves as becoming better and better Christians, achieving greater and greater success in devotion, morals, service and witnessing. This would be quite challenging and satisfying to human nature. Such a way of achievement, however, contains the seeds of sinfulness within itself, for it still revolves around ourselves. God is still left on the periphery of life, to be used as a lever to help self achieve what it desires. Since such a way does not make it possible for us to honor God as God, it cannot break the power of sin.

We are not even allowed any heroism for choosing the Way of the cross, for the cross itself appears to be utter folly even to us until it has captivated us. Thus God is honored as God and the necessary relationship between Creator and creature prevails.

> *Enter by the narrow gate; for the gate is wide and the way is easy, that leads to destruction, and those who enter by it are many. For the gate is narrow and the way is hard, that leads to life, and those who find it are few (Matthew 7:13-14).*

CHAPTER SIX

The Flesh and the Spirit

*T*HIS *CHAPTER deals with two particularly significant New Testament passages, the seventh and
eighth chapters of Romans. Those who have previously
considered these passages and their practical significance
for Christian living should find this chapter meaningful.
If you have not done much reading in the New Testament,
you may wish to skip this chapter and come back to it
later. It is not necessary to read it in order to understand
the chapters that follow. However, if you do not find it
difficult to understand, by all means read it, for it is closely
related to what we have already been discussing. It will be
helpful to read it with your Bible open to the seventh and
eight chapters of Romans in order to follow the references
which are given. It is particularly important for those who
have already considered the relationship between the flesh
and the Spirit to read this chapter before going on, to make
sure they are giving the same emphasis that Paul does to
the place of the cross in this relationship.*

No greater admission of spiritual helplessness than is
expressed in Romans 7:15-25 can be found anywhere:

*15 I do not understand my own actions. For I do not
do what I want, but I do the very thing I hate. 16 Now*

if I do what I do not want, I agree that the law is good.
[17] So then it is no longer I that do it, but sin which
dwells within me.[18] For I know that nothing good
dwells within me, that is, in my flesh. I can will what
is right, but I cannot do it. [19] For I do not do the good I
want, but the evil I do not want is what I do. [20] Now
if I do what I do not want, it is no longer I that do it,
but sin which dwells within me.

[21] So I find it to be a law that when I want to do
right, evil lies close at hand. [22] For I delight in the law
of God, in my inmost self, [23] but I see in my members
another law at war with the law of my mind and mak-
ing me captive to the law of sin which dwells in my
members.[24] Wretched man that I am! Who will deliver
me from this body of death? [25] Thanks be to God
through Jesus Christ our Lord! So then, I of myself
serve the law of God with my mind, but with my flesh
I serve the law of sin.

This statement continues without interruption in
Romans 8:1-4 in a contrasting note of complete freedom:

[1] There is therefore now no condemnation for those
who are in Christ Jesus. [2] For the law of the Spirit of
life in Christ Jesus has set me free from the law of sin
and death. [3] For God has done what the law, weakened
by the flesh, could not do: sending his own Son in the
likeness of sinful flesh and for sin, he condemned sin
in the flesh, [4] in order that the just requirement of the
law might be fulfilled in us, who walk not according
to the flesh but according to the Spirit.

The first passage deals with captivity, the second deals
with freedom. The first deals with the law of sin and
death, the second deals with the law of the Spirit of life.
The two seem to be poles apart. However, Paul passes

from one to the other without any break whatsoever, as though he were speaking of the same conditions in both passages. If we disregard the heading at chapter eight, which is not a part of the original text, we go directly from one to the other as though they were one.

We shall begin the discussion of these passages with a consideration of what Paul means by "the flesh." This term is used to describe everything about us which is earthly and mortal. The flesh includes more than the body and is not identified with the body. The flesh is that attribute of human beings which makes life revolve around self. The chief concern of the flesh is the preservation and satisfaction of self. The "sinful passions" (Romans 7:5) reside in the flesh. If we will bear in mind that the basic definition of sin is to refuse to honor God as God (Chapter Three), it will be clear that the sinfulness of the desires of the flesh consists in that they insist on being satisfied even in defiance of what God has commanded. The desires themselves are not necessarily sinful. The sinfulness of the flesh lies in the fact that its concern for self is not subordinate to the authority of God. The flesh knows no god but self.

There is a constant moral battle within the flesh itself. For instance, the flesh desires comfort. It also desires approval. It may tempt one person to steal a large sum of money to make himself more comfortable. It may keep another person from stealing because it fears disapproval

if he is caught. The flesh may tempt a person to adultery.
At the same time it may tend to keep him from adultery
because it detests the stigma of social disapproval or the
discomfort of guilt feelings. The flesh appreciates aes-
thetic values, feelings of sympathy, desires for self-improvement, and religious and moral living in so far as they are
satisfying to self. (Philippians 3:4-6, for instance, reveals
how much moral and religious interest may reside in the
flesh.)

In Romans 7:15-25, Paul is not dealing with this moral
struggle within the flesh itself. In this passage he rejects
everything about the flesh and declares that "nothing
good" dwells in it (Romans 7:18). Whether the flesh
incites us to morality or to immorality, self is still central,
and God is not honored as God in either case.

All our relationships with the world are through the
flesh. Our senses are like lines of communication between
the flesh and the world around us. All that is of the flesh
will pass away with the world (I John 2:16-17). The
New Testament offers no promise of improvement for the
flesh. As we shall see, it has another way of dealing with it.

The most emphatic thing that Paul says in Romans
7:15-25 is that in his real self, he is free from sin. It is
highly significant that in the midst of so much emphasis on
sin and captivity, Paul twice comes to the conclusion that
he himself does not sin. It is sin which dwells within him.
In Romans 7:16-17 he says, "Now if I do what I do not

want, I agree that the law is good. So then it is no longer I that do it, but sin which dwells within me." Again, in Romans 7:20, he repeats the same statement almost word for word.

Here is a man who delights in the law of God. In spite of this fact, however, he still says, "I know that nothing good dwells within me, that is, in my flesh" (Romans 7:18). He is a man who has turned against his flesh and has accepted the fact that his flesh is sinful. Yet, in his real self he is free from sin. It is no longer he who sins, but sin dwelling in him. As we have already seen, this is exactly what Paul has been saying throughout the entire Epistle to the Romans about the attitude of a person who comes face to face with the Cross of Christ. When we see ourselves as sinners, for whom there is no other hope than the mercy of God, the power of sin is broken and we are free from sin.

It has been suggested that the seventh chapter of Romans should be applied to Paul in his pre-conversion state, when he was a self-righteous Pharisee. During that time he had been zealous for the law, and he could have said that he delighted in the law of God. It is true that the unconverted person does have a moral struggle. However, before his conversion, all Paul's delight in the law of God was in the flesh, because of the gain it brought to him personally (See Philippians 3:4-7). In the seventh chapter of Romans, on the other hand, he is opposed to the flesh, and his delight in the law of God is completely contrary to the flesh. Therefore, his primary reference, at least, must not be to his pre-conversion experience.

The seventh chapter of Romans is definitely not a picture of a split personality. It is the description of a man who is unreservedly committed to God and is so opposed to sin that he can even look objectively upon it when it appears in his own flesh. He is completely agreed within himself in his opposition to the flesh. The flesh is not a part of his real nature. If it were, he could not be so undividedly opposed to it. He has accepted the fact that in his flesh he is a sinner. This fact distresses him, because it creates a situation to which he is opposed, but it does not frustrate him. It humbles him and causes him to glory in the cross, for both the necessity and sufficiency of Christ's death on the cross are vindicated by what he sees in his flesh. Therefore, as he looks upon the sinfulness of his flesh, he turns with thanks to God through Jesus Christ, for His mercy in removing the condemnation of sin, and says, "There is therefore now no condemnation for those who are in Christ Jesus."

This brings us to the question: Can a person be living a normal Christian life when he is as sinful as he is described in Romans 7:15-25? Does not God intend that Christians shall be more successful in dealing with the flesh than this?

This passage is often said to describe a subnormal state of Christian experience in contrast with the eighth chapter which is said to portray the normal state of a Christian. This interpretation does, however, present certain difficulties. Paul does not indicate anywhere that it is his intention to set the two passages in contrast. He does not tell when the subnormal state changes to normal or how such a normal state is to be reached. Such an interpretation would be more acceptable if he would speak in the past tense in Romans 7:15-25 and in the present tense in Romans 8:1-4, as though he had once been defeated but has now learned the secret of victory. However, he does not speak in this way. Romans 7:15-25, which describes his sense of great sinfulness, is written in the present tense. Yet, when he speaks of being set free, in Romans 8:2, he speaks in the past tense, as though his sense of sinfulness followed his being set free.

The saintliest Christians often see themselves most clearly described in Romans 7:15-25; and sometimes, when they are taught that it is not normal for them to look upon themselves in this way, their peace of mind is destroyed and they begin an endless search for something different. There have been cases where those who have tried to lead them on to such victorious living know less of the grace of God than they, for it is possible to profess a kind of freedom from sin which is really only blindness to sin.

Let us remember that this is a man's estimate of himself. The significance of the personal pronoun, "I," is that Paul is describing the way he looks upon himself. Paul could never speak this way about another person, nor could any other person speak this way about Paul. In relationship to the world around him, and in relationship to the moral standards of either Judaism or Christianity, Paul lived an exemplary life. Paul said even of his former life, before his conversion, that, according to the righteousness under the law, he was blameless (Philippians 3:6). The record shows Paul to be of sound character, both as a Pharisee and as a Christian. The reason that Paul saw himself as such a sinner was not that he was so uniquely bad. It was that his standard of moral righteousness was being constantly raised as he walked with the Lord. The real significance of this passage is that, in spite of the fact that he sees himself to be so sinful, he can still give thanks to God, for there is still no condemnation to those who are in Christ Jesus (Romans 7:25-8:1).

Paul also says of himself, "One thing I do, forgetting what lies behind and straining forward to what lies ahead, I press on toward the goal for the prize of the upward call of God in Christ Jesus" (Philippians 3:13-14). Paul's only standard of comparison was the goal of perfection in Christ. Is there any other way that a person with such a goal could see himself than the way Paul sees himself in the seventh chapter of Romans?

If Paul were looking backward, he might say, "As I look back over my past life, I can see how evil I was. In comparison with what I was, I have now, with God's help, become quite an ideal person." Since, however, he blots his past from his memory and looks forward, he can only say, "In comparison with what is to come, I am evil. In my flesh dwells no good thing."

Charles Wesley follows the same thought in his great hymn, "Jesus, Lover of My Soul":

> "Just and holy is Thy name,
> I am all unrighteousness,
> Vile and full of sin I am,
> Thou art full of truth and grace."

No one would interpret Paul as saying that he never did *any* good deed, or that he did *all* the evil that he hated. When he said, "For I do not do the good I want, but the evil I do not want is what I do," he was simply saying that there was good which he desired to do but which he did not do; and there was evil which he did even though he hated it; there was a mixture of evil in all that he did. As Paul walked with Jesus, he became increasingly sensitive to the call of God upon his life, and increasingly sensitive both to righteousness and to sin. He did not compare himself with what he was before he was converted or what he was even now. He forgot what lay behind and compared himself only with God's call upon him. From this viewpoint, his sense of sinfulness is completely logical.

Christian victory does not lift us to a place where we are no longer conscious of sin. Each one of us is conscious of mixed motives, even in our highest efforts; of good that we leave undone, and of evil which we should not be doing. This is true of those who seem to be the most victorious Christians.

We may anticipate another problem in Romans 7:24 where Paul says, "Wretched man that I am! Who will deliver me from this body of death?" Can we accept wretchedness to be normal Christian experience?

Paul demonstrates elsewhere that joy and sorrow, peace and conflict, triumph and distress dwell at the same time in his soul. As an example, in Romans 8:37 he triumphantly asserts, "In all these things we are more than conquerors through Him who loved us." Yet, just a few sentences farther on, in Romans 9:2, he says, "I have great sorrow and unceasing anguish in my heart." Here triumph exists side by side with anguish for his unconverted countrymen.

The wretchedness which Paul expresses in Romans 7:24 is due to his desire to be delivered from what he calls "this body of death." We need not try to solve the difficult problem of the exact meaning of this expression. It is obvious that he is longing to be free from the limitations which the flesh places upon him. The important thing to remember is that we have the same kind of expression in Romans 8:23, "we ourselves, who have the firstfruits of the Spirit, groan inwardly as we wait for adoption as sons, the redemption of our bodies." Here he says that the Spirit produces an inward groaning for the glory of the future life for the Christian. The "wretchedness" of Romans

7:24 can likewise be interpreted as the inward groaning of intense longing for the glory of the day when he will be set free from the flesh in the resurrection. The entire New Testament bears out the fact that the Christian is filled with a longing for the glory that will one day be his. There is an agony about an intense longing that can very well be expressed as "wretchedness." It seems most natural to interpret Paul's "wretchedness" in Romans 7:24 as another expression of the intensity of this longing.

Another question may be raised by Romans 7:25: It is easy to accept the expression, "I of myself serve the law of God with my mind," as normal Christian experience; but it is more difficult to accept the expression, "but with my flesh I serve the law of sin," as being normal to a Christian. Is not this the admission of a defeated Christian? In reply, we may ask: Where in the entire New Testament is there any promise that the flesh will ever serve anything but the law of sin? The fact is that Paul was not living according to the flesh, but whatever was motivated by his flesh was done for self, and the law of sin is the law that puts self before God. This is the only law that the flesh knows. Paul was only being realistic. There is no Christian whose flesh does not serve the law of sin by tempting him, at every opportunity it has, to put self before God.

Let us now consider the eighth chapter. It begins with the words, "There is therefore now no condemnation for those who are in Christ Jesus. For the law of the Spirit of life in Christ Jesus has set me free from the law of sin and death." The law of sin and death is the law which requires the flesh to seek to perpetuate and to satisfy itself even in defiance of God. It is the law of death because death always accompanies sin. Paul does not say, "The Spirit of life in Christ Jesus *will* make me free from the law of sin and death." This is something which he says the Spirit has already done. It is not an advanced achievement in Christian living to be free from the law of sin and death; it is something which has already happened to the Christian. This is the whole point of the eighth chapter. He is saying that the Spirit has set him free from the law of sin and death in the sense that it is possible for the inward man to delight in the law of God, to recognize the sinfulness of the flesh and to turn against it; that is, in the sense that he has already described in the seventh chapter. Paul claims freedom from the law of sin and death, but he never claims freedom from the flesh itself.

As Paul specifically states in Romans 8:1-2, the freedom which he is describing is freedom from the condemnation of sin. We first obtained this freedom when we came to God in repentance and received His pardon. It was the freedom we obtained at the cross. Therefore, the consciousness of this freedom will continue in our experience when we continue in the same attitude we took when we first came to the cross: that is, in the attitude of brokenness, recognizing that we are still sinners and dependent constantly on God's pardon. This is precisely the attitude which Paul is describing in Romans 7:15-25. Never does he describe freedom from sin in a way which permits us to look upon ourselves as anything else than sinners.

It is interesting to notice how in Romans 8:1-4, Paul uses the plural pronouns "those" and "us." Between these two sentences, he returns to the pronoun, "me" (Romans 8:2). It is as though he were saying that the Spirit of life in Christ Jesus has set the "me" of those who are in Christ Jesus free from the law of sin and death. The "me" of Romans 7:23, which includes the whole man with his fleshly members, is being brought continually into captivity to the law of sin. However, it is a captivity in which the inward man, or "the inmost self" has no part, for the "me" of Romans 8:2, which is "the inmost self," has been set free from the law of sin and death, and delights unreservedly in the law of God.

The power described in Romans 8:1-4 is clearly indicated to be the power of the cross. Paul says that, "Sending his own Son in the likeness of sinful flesh and for sin, he [God] condemned sin in the flesh, in order that the just requirement of the law might be fulfilled in us, who walk not according to the flesh but according to the Spirit." God condemned sin by means of the death of Christ on the cross. The reason God condemned sin (that is, the reason Christ died on the cross), Paul says, was that the just requirement of the law might be fulfilled in those who walk not according to the flesh but according to the Spirit. The

Holy Spirit is prominent in the eighth chapter of Romans in order to emphasize that it is He who makes it effective, but the power is that of the death of Christ on the cross. The cross is central in the eighth chapter of Romans just as it is in the third chapter. Therefore, the freedom described in the eighth chapter is the freedom enjoyed by those who repent and trust in God's pardon, for, as we have seen, the purpose of the cross is to make pardon available to those who repent.

This brings us to the question, "What does Paul mean by walking according to the Spirit?" A man recently said to me, "I could be victorious as a Christian if I could only learn to walk according to the Spirit."

Walking according to the Spirit is the fundamental requirement of all Christian experience. This is stated not only in the eighth chapter of Romans but also in Galatians 5:16, and it is implied in a number of other instances. Walking according to the Spirit must therefore be the kindergarten of Christian experience. Since everything depends on walking according to the Spirit, this must be a very simple thing, of which every Christian is fully capable.

We have a confirmation, in Galatians 3:3, of the elementary nature of the Christian's relationship to the Spirit; "Are you so foolish? Having begun with the Spirit, are you now ending with the flesh?" Paul is reprimanding the Galatian Christians for returning to the flesh and continuing their Christian life in dependence on human achievement. He says that this is foolish since they began with the Spirit. To walk according to the Spirit, therefore, can only mean to continue the Christian life in the same way in which we began. We began the Christian life at the cross, in repentance and dependence on God's pardon. As we have seen, it was the Holy Spirit who made it possible for us to do this by convincing us of our sinfulness. Walking according to the Spirit, therefore, means that we continue, in the same broken and contrite attitude, to take the sinner's place and to depend entirely on God's mercy and pardon. The Spirit of God has been given to us to lead us on in such an attitude (Romans 8:14).

Walking according to the Spirit is not an achievement in the Christian life. It is something we began when we were converted, and the only way to restore the walk according to the Spirit is to return to the attitude we had then. It is exactly what the Lord was calling the Ephesian Church to do when He said, "Repent and do the works you did at first" (Revelation 2:5).

Our final problem concerns Romans 8:3-4, in which Paul says, "For God has done what the law, weakened by the flesh, could not do: sending his own Son in the likeness of sinful flesh and for sin, he condemned sin in the flesh, in order that the just requirement of the law might be fulfilled in us, who walk not according to the flesh but according to the Spirit."

What is "the just requirement," or, as otherwise trans-
lated, "the righteousness" of the law? It does not mean that
every demand of the law will be fulfilled in the absolute
perfection of the Christian's life. This would be a hopeless
ideal, which for most of us could lead to nothing but
despair. Let us consider this in the light of the first part of
the sentence which speaks of God condemning sin in the
flesh. God condemned sin through the death of Christ on
the cross, that the sinner might be free from every charge
that is against him and be declared completely righteous.
When the sinner is declared righteous, every requirement
of the law is thereby fulfilled in him. There is nothing in
this passage or in any of the teachings of Paul to indicate
that the just requirement of the law is fulfilled in the perfection of the Christian's character. God has canceled
everything He holds against him because Christ condemned sin. Thus, the just requirement of the law is fulfilled in him by Christ when he comes in repentance and
faith to the cross.

We always keep coming back to the same point in
everything Paul says. At every turn the cross stands before
us again. We may think that we have passed beyond it,
when suddenly we find ourselves approaching it from a
slightly different viewpoint. Paul says one thing, then he
looks back upon it in retrospect, and this leads him to
approach it from another position.

In the third and fourth chapters of Romans Paul
describes how we are declared righteous when we recog-

nize our sinfulness and trust in what Christ has done by
dying for us. Looking back on this experience from the
viewpoint of the sixth chapter, he describes it as dying
to sin. He then tells us we should continue to consider ourselves dead to sin and alive to God. From what he has said
previously, we understand that this means we are to continue to recognize that we are sinners who are dependent
on God's pardon. Sin has no more power to condemn us
for we are not under the law but under grace. Both dying
to sin and living for God mean continual repentance.

In the seventh chapter he describes graphically what it
really means for a person to look upon himself as a sinner.
He, himself, in his inmost self is free from sin, but in his
flesh he is a sinner. Yet, because of the cross, there is no
condemnation to them who are in Christ Jesus. Then, in
the eighth chapter, he looks back on the seventh chapter
and says that it was the Spirit of life in Christ Jesus who
has produced the attitude of the seventh chapter, in which
a man is so free from sin that he can turn against it even
in his own flesh. Because of what Christ has done, there is
no condemnation to those who are in Him. The Spirit has
set them free because God condemned sin by sending
Christ to die on the cross. By this means the just requirement of the law is fulfilled in them; not by their own character, but because God has declared them to be righteous.
He never actually mentions the cross by name, but in
everything the cross is central, and its unique logic prevails over everything that he says. In fact, without what

he says about the significance of the death of Christ, the entire epistle is completely meaningless.

Christ's death on the cross produces a balance in our attitude toward righteousness and sin. We cannot look so lightly on sin that we disregard it, for we are in agreement with God even about our own sinfulness. At the same time its presence in our flesh is not so frustrating that we are thrown into despair. It is not so unnatural that we do not dare to admit its presence.

No greater handicap faces the Church of today than its appearance of superficiality. The non-believing world which lives right at the doors of the church sees the failings that Christians themselves often fear to face. There is little in this unrealistic picture to attract the world to Christ.

One of the reasons for this superficiality is a kind of feeling among Christians that they are not supposed to be sinners. This is deeper than just a wrong conception of Christian teaching. It goes right down to the perversity of the human heart, which refuses to accept its own sinfulness.

This leaves Christians only two alternatives: (1) They may make light of their failings and dismiss them as faults common to all humanity. They may speak of them as sins without accepting them as being really sinful. (2) On the other hand, they may recognize their sinfulness inwardly, but, because such sinfulness is considered to be so abnormal to Christian experience, they must try to suppress it and to hide it even from themselves. This also requires them to build thick walls around themselves in order to present the best appearance possible to their fellow Christians and to the world. The result is a great load of suppressed guilt which makes the hope of abundant and joyous living a hollow mockery.

Christians then only break down under tremendous pressure, and when someone does repent, he himself feels that he is going through a very special crisis in his experience, while others hail him as a wanderer returning from a far country and commend him warmly for his courage. It is difficult for Christians to accept this as perfectly normal Christian experience, which should be going on all the time under the guidance of the Holy Spirit.

When Christians begin repenting, it causes them to lose some of their stiffness and stuffiness, and the world sees that Christianity has reality. When the non-believing world sees that Christians themselves recognize that they are as great sinners as they obviously appear to be, and that Christianity has the power to bring them to repentance, one of the greatest stumbling blocks to unbelievers is immediately removed. Jesus Christ, and Him crucified, constantly in the center of our Christian experience, will bring this to pass.

> "O Cross that liftest up my head,
> I dare not ask to hide from Thee;

I lay in dust life's glory dead,
And from the ground there blossoms red,
    Life that shall endless be."

CHAPTER SEVEN

The Christian's Warfare

U P TO THIS POINT, a certain militant note which is characteristic of New Testament Christianity may seem to be missing. It may seem that we are making Christian experience too serene and colorless. Striving and struggling all seem to be removed. In putting Christian experience on a level where the weakest may benefit by it, have we not removed the challenge to the strong? All we need to do is confess our sinfulness and accept God's pardon. Will this not make Christians indolent and self-indulgent? What incentives are left for piety and growth?

There are, of course, concepts of Christianity which invite us to relax and be carried comfortably, without conflict or concern, in peaceful quietness through all the battles of life to the restful shores of our heavenly home. Such concepts are not correct, and they do not produce spiritual health.

We have, however, been speaking about repenting, not relaxing. Although repentance produces a relaxation of conflicting tensions, there is a vast difference between relaxation and repentance. Complete relaxation is death, but to be completely repentant is to be abundantly alive in Christ.

This matter of accepting ourselves as sinners, needing God's pardon, is no mechanical formula for victory. No man can speak lightly when he says that he is a sinner. If he says it lightly, he is speaking in self-justification and he has not yet really seen his sinfulness. The attitude of "Wretched man that I am" will always accompany the recognition of our sinfulness. We have not eliminated the Christian's warfare; we have simply moved the battle-ground into the area of the cross. It is in this area that victory has been equally assured to all Christians. This is the only area where we can battle in the Spirit, with the full assurance that in the end we will come out triumphant. Our victory will not, however, reveal to us that we are such successful Christians. It will reveal to us that we are sinners.

A minister had just concluded a service which had been a great blessing. God had brought several to repentance. Many had shaken his hand and expressed enthusiastic and sincere appreciation for his message and the release it brought to them.

He came back to his room with a sense of great satisfaction and with the warm glow of success upon his heart. He was keenly conscious that God had used him. He began to hope and pray fervently within his heart that God would continue to use him. He knew that he could be used only if he were humbled, so he began to pray for great humility in order that he might continue to be used. He considered the people who had been blessed that evening, thinking with satisfaction of how each one had been touched. He began to think of how they would speak of him to others in terms of appreciation. In all of this he had no peace. The Spirit brought him face to face with the fact that he was only a sinner. This brought a pious response of thanksgiving to God that He could use a mere sinner to be such a blessing. Still he had no peace. The Spirit prompted him to recognize, here and now, that he was incapable of any good, that in the very goodness in which God had used him as an instrument, self was claiming a share.

The hours went by as God struggled with him to recognize that the warm glow which brought him such satisfaction had in it all the seeds of sinfulness. It was not a struggle to overcome this feeling of satisfaction. That would have been far beyond him. The Spirit was merely urging him to recognize it as being further evidence of his need of the mercy of God, and to turn against it. Finally the Spirit won the battle with self. In brokenness he confessed that he was still a sinner, in as great need of repentance as any with whom he had dealt that evening. He could no longer thank God for using him. He could only thank God for a Saviour who died on a cross for such as he. This was no mere mechanical formula to him. It reached down into the very depths of his soul. His victory consisted in his being able to accept himself as a mere sinner.

This must be the kind of spiritual exercise Paul refers to in I Corinthians 9:26-27, "I do not run aimlessly, I do not box as one beating the air; but I pommel my body and

subdue it, lest after preaching to others I myself should
be disqualified."

This statement could either mean that Paul subdued his
body in a herioc effort to drive himself to achieve certain
standards of Christian living, or it could mean that he subdued it in order to force himself to accept his own sinfulness and continual need of pardon. We get his correct
meaning from the last phrase of the sentence, "lest after
preaching to others I myself should be disqualified." In
other words, he subjected himself to his own preaching.
Everything in Paul's preaching, of course, centered about
the cross. Since the cross is the place of repentance and
pardon, we may understand him to be saying that his great
struggle was to subdue his body and to force himself to see
his own sinfulness in repentance and to rest only on God's
pardon. Everything Paul seems to say about self-discipline
in this section must be interpreted in the light of his emphasis on the cross.

This kind of a struggle arises out of the fact that there
are really two kinds of religion. One is the religion of
achievement. This is the kind of religion that we support
and defend and uphold because it calls us to do the best
we can. It challenges us to live so nobly that we may have
the satisfaction of knowing that we have done well. The
other is the religion of grace. This is the kind of religion
that supports and upholds us. It continually reveals us to be
needy sinners and it offers us the grace and mercy of God.

There has always been conflict between these two. Those who are familiar with the Bible and with Christian history will recognize this conflict in Ishmael and Isaac, Esau and Jacob, the law from Mt. Sinai and grace from Mt. Zion, the Pharisees and Jesus, the legalists and Paul, etc.

It is easy to see why the religion of accomplishment would oppose the religion of grace. It seems so noble to support and uphold one's religious faith and to keep it alive. It seems so satisfying to self to become conscious of religious achievements. The high ideals of such a religion seem to challenge us to become courageous and devout.

On the other hand, those who embrace the religion of grace seem so free, so captivated by their faith, so spontaneous in the discharging of their responsibility that there must be something wrong. When one person has labored and struggled for years to achieve certain spiritual goals, it is difficult to see how another person can, without any effort on his part, enter immediately into the enjoyment of every spiritual blessing. Furthermore, the religion of grace seems to attract the common multitudes who often appear to have little sense of responsibility or inclination to discipline themselves.

We must remember that it was the cultured, respectable people who opposed Paul. They were afraid that the unique standards which were upheld by the few people who found satisfaction in the rigorous disciplines of their religion would be endangered by Paul's message of freedom. We must remember that even he was accused, though falsely, of making his religion an excuse for sin (Romans 3:8).

Paul, himself, must constantly have faced the temptation to compromise with the religion of accomplishment, to respond to the call to a religious experience that offered greater incentives for personal achievement and more satisfaction to self. However, he was aware that he, himself, must also stand as a sinner before the cross which he preached to others.

This same struggle goes on within our own souls. Self will always seek satisfaction in the religion of human accomplishment and achievement. However, we know that the nature of the cross is such that in its presence we can have nothing in which to boast. We must be sinners whose only glory is Christ and what He has done. Although the religion of accomplishment appeals to us, it also keeps us in bondage, for we are never able to accomplish enough to satisfy self. On the other hand, though the religion of grace offers no satisfaction for self, it releases us into complete freedom. Just as we are, we may come, if we will only face the fact of our sinfulness and accept God's pardon. It is the struggle to see ourselves only as sinners and to trust only in God's mercy that constitutes the Christian's warfare.

If this is the case, we may ask what our attitude should be toward the ethical instructions and appeals to righteous living in the New Testament, including the teachings of

Jesus. These instructions, properly interpreted, represent God's will for His people. Therefore, if we are truly Christian, we will delight in them and desire nothing greater than to conform to the ethical principles which they convey. It will be our guiding principle to obey the will of God in everything we do. The upward call to noble and holy living will always find a warm response in our hearts.

At the same time, we should neither be frustrated by our failures nor rejoice in our accomplishments. God is not a condemning critic, sitting in harsh judgment on every mistake we make. Neither is He a proud parent who, like a human father, is greatly pleased at his child's efforts to achieve. He is in the unique position of being our Heavenly Father, who has given His only Son to redeem us from the power of sin, which has its roots in self. He knows our every weakness; He sympathizes with our every failure, and He loves us with a love that is beyond expression.

Our imperfections will, however, reveal to us that we are still dependent on the benefits of the cross, and will produce an attitude of penitence and a broken spirit. Disciplined living is important to Christianity, and Christian living has many disciplines. However, all these disciplines are dependent on the one discipline of the cross. The discipline of the cross brings us constantly to our need of repentance.

It is contrary to Chistian principles to set up rigorous self-disciplinary projects just for the purpose of teaching self the habit of submission. Such practices either result in self being glorified by proving that it can conform to such disciplines or they result in a sense of defeat and guilt because self will not conform. In either case self proves itself triumphant. Paul speaks of such disciplines and regulations in Colossians 2:23, "These have indeed an appearance of wisdom in promoting rigor of devotion and self-abasement and severity to the body, but they are of no value in checking the indulgence of the flesh." Blessed is the man who has learned to bring self to see its own sinfulness and need of the cross. All other necessary disciplines in the Christian life are dependent on this.

The same thing is true about God's will for us in relation to our responsibilities to our church and our fellow Christians, to the missionary call, to opportunities for witnessing and Christian activities, to the Christian vision of the need of the entire world. In many cases, we will not be certain about God's will, but if we cease our striving and live in a submissive attitude, we may confidently expect that He will lead us. Christians are not to look upon themselves just as individuals. The Church is a unit, in which the Holy Spirit directs Christians together. There must be submissiveness, not only to God, but also to one another, for the Spirit is building up the entire Church together. The work of the Spirit in the Church is possible only where there is a submissive attitude through broken and contrite hearts.

When we walk in brokenness and repentance, accepting what Christ did on the cross, we may depend on the Spirit of God to produce the fruit of sound Christian character. "But the fruit of the Spirit is love, joy, peace, patience, kindness, goodness, faithfulness, gentleness, self-control" (Galatians 5:22-23).

This fruit is not produced by striving for a better life. It is not something of which we ourselves need to become conscious. Those around us will benefit by it and God will be glorified. Although Christianity has theological principles, Christian living is not just the application of principles, and it is not lived in a theological world. It is in the daily experiences of practical relationships with other people, earning a living, forming friendships, visiting, making decisions, in the home, on the job, in the school, in the various community projects in which the Christian participates, etc., that it must exert its strongest influence. We live among people of flesh and blood who know little or nothing about the theological significance of the spiritual struggle.

Christians who try to drive themselves in a conscious effort toward the attaining of higher ideals in order to make an impression for God, will appear stilted and unnatural to the world around them and will have little influence. No one is impressed by laborious efforts at self-discipline, but a life that is alive with Christlike qualities, so natural to the Christian that he is unconscious of them, has a profound effect upon people to whom Christ-likeness is only an unattainable ideal. When we live in an attitude of brokenness and submission to Christ it is like breaking up the soil of our hearts so that the spiritual life may be fruitful. For us it is sufficient to be conscious only that we are sinners who need the grace and mercy of God.

If, however, we can never look upon ourselves as making any progress, will we not grow discouraged and tend to give up? What is the use of going on unless we can see some improvement? The answer to this question is that if we were living for self we would require something to encourage self. However, the Spirit, according to whom we live, is not motivated by our self-improvement.

There is one sense, however, in which we may expect to see spiritual progress. We may expect to become increasingly sensitive to sin and righteousness. The sins of which we find ourselves conscious will be new sins, which we did not recognize before. Some, at least, of the old sins will no longer continue to tempt us.

We must remember that this is no mechanical formula. It is Christ Himself who is redeeming us, and we shall need His presence constantly.

When we live this way, the Christian life will never grow monotonous and cold. We shall never speak about how much more blessed were the early days of our Christian experience. Instead of needing Christ less and less as we become more firmly entrenched in the forms of Christianity, the passing years will make us increasingly conscious of our need of Christ, for they will make us more and more sensitive to the things within us for which He died.

"More than conquerors" is a superlative expression of triumph. If we were not so familiar with Paul, we would expect him to say that we are more than conquerors through the continual influence of the high ideals of Christianity, through Christ's power to help us overcome temptation, through the disciplinary effects of Christianity upon our lives, or through some special achievement in Christian living. Knowing what we now do about Paul, however, it would surprise us to have him say any of these. We would expect him to say precisely what he does, "In all these things we are more than conquerors through Him who loved us. For I am sure that neither death, nor life, nor angels, nor principalities, nor things present, nor things to come, nor powers, nor height, nor depth, nor anything else in all creation, will be able to separate us from the love of God in Christ Jesus our Lord" (Romans 8:37-39).

It is the love of God, revealed to us through Jesus Christ, which has made us more than conquerors. It is His love that motivated Him to give His Son to die on the cross. It is His love that prevails over our sinfulness and draws us to Himself. It is His love that conquers our hearts so that we turn against our own sinful selves. It is His love that motivates us to worship and serve Him.

The real victory is to recognize how much we need His love, that it has prevailed to provide redemption in spite of the sinfulness that still persists in us, that nothing will separate us from His love. This is to be *more than conquerors.*

CHAPTER EIGHT

A New Relationship

JESUS CHRIST also makes possible a new kind of relationship with others. Most of life is dependent on our associations with our fellow men. No enjoyment is complete unless it can be shared with someone else. No mental agony is more distressing than the feeling of complete loneliness. If we remove from life those values which are dependent on our relationship with others, we have very little left.

Yet, man's sinfulness has marred his relationship with others. As we have already seen, the essence of sinfulness is to refuse to honor God as God because life revolves around ourselves. Each one lives in a world in which he is at the center. Therefore he can find no one to share the world as he sees it, for all others must look upon life from their own viewpoint. The result is a great loneliness within the heart of each person. Sin, therefore, is a great separator.

Since everyone sees life from a different viewpoint, complete understanding among men is impossible. The best we can do is to reach a compromise between what we would like and what other people would like. Such compromises are the basis of agreement between labor and management. They result in many of our governmental regulations. They are behind many of our social customs and usages.

In these compromises we recognize the advantages of foregoing certain immediate selfish pleasures in order to enjoy more permanent and lasting satisfaction in harmony with others. We may, for instance, refrain from taking advantage of a competitor when he is in a tight spot for we prefer the more lasting satisfaction of having the good will of the community. We may refrain from speeding even when no officer is nearby, for we prefer the satisfaction of having obeyed the law over the possible distress of having caused an accident through our own unlawfulness. We may lend our tools to our neighbor even though he neglects to return them, for we prefer not to have him consider us unneighborly. However, if we can think of an excuse which seems good enough to keep him from considering us unneighborly even though we do not lend him the tools, we are more than likely to consider ourselves fortunate.

"I would never think of neglecting my aged mother," said a faithful daughter. "Why, I would have a bad conscience to my dying day." A comfortable conscience was, of course, her chief concern. The human traits of sympathy, kindness and good will are highly developed and complex emotions which bring us great personal satisfaction. Self is always at the center. There should be nothing particularly disillusioning about this state of affairs. It is the inevitable effect of man's sinfulness.

Jesus said, "Whatever you wish that men would do to you, do so to them; for this is the law and the prophets" (Matthew 7:12). When he said this, He knew He was speaking to sinners whose life revolved around self and who could best be motivated to treat others decently by thinking about how they themselves would like to be treated. He never even hinted that they would be saved from their sinfulness by obeying this command. It merely serves to help selfish sinners get along with other selfish sinners. Furthermore, He said that this principle prevails throughout the whole law of God and the teachings of the prophets.

This statement of Jesus is contained in the Sermon on the Mount, which is perhaps the most fundamental discourse on human ethics and relationships He ever annunciated. At the conclusion of the Sermon on the Mount, Jesus emphasized the importance of doing as He had said by an illustration of two houses, one built on the sand and the other on the rock. The person who does as Jesus has said is likened to a man whose house will weather the most severe storm because it has been "founded on the rock" (Matthew 7:24-27).

It is a sad commentary on human nature that Jesus found it necessary to conclude this magnificent discourse with an appeal to the personal advantage of having a house that will not crumble. When each person lives ethically, seeking the best for his neighbor, because, by so doing he will be strengthening the foundations of his own house, he is still a selfish man. A society built on these precepts alone may be an orderly society, but it will be a society of lonely people, for the chief concern of each person will be his own house.

Jesus, of course, was realistic. He knew that the life of every person revolved around self when He made this appeal. The fact that this discourse closes with this kind of an illustration is evidence that men cannot be saved from sin by following principles and commandments. Sin continues to separate, life continues to revolve around each individual, and human relationships which satisfy the deepest needs of the soul for fellowship are impossible.

Since life for each one of us revolves around himself and each one of us looks upon life from a different perspective, disharmony is the normal condition. Harmony is achieved only by effort, because men have learned through the centuries that it is more advantageous to live in harmony with others. When the effort to maintain harmonious relationships becomes too great, there is a breach. The result is misunderstanding, offense, disagreement, factions and even violence. The world is full of such breaches. Self is all too often unable to reach a compromise with other selves, all of whom see life from a different viewpoint.

What is missing in human relationships is a common perspective, from which all men can look at life, so that each person naturally seeks his place among his fellow men in relation to this common perspective. If this could be achieved, harmony rather than disharmony would be normal, and ideal human relationships would be a natural condition rather than a tense compromise.

If God is honored as God, He will be at the center of life, and all of life will be seen from His perspective. This is the true common perspective. Our sinfulness makes this impossible. It is more than a mere trite generalization, therefore, to say that it is man's sinfulness that makes ideal human relationships impossible.

The redemptive work of Christ includes removing the obstacles to ideal human relationships and setting up a new relationship which is unique among men.

We have already made it quite clear that Christians continue to be sinners. Life for them also continues to revolve around self. For this reason, relationships even among Christians are not ideal. Breaches, factions and divisions are all too common. Christians, however, must recognize that they are sinners, and accept God's pardon. Every evidence of the self-centered life proves God to be right in calling them sinners and should bring them to repentance at the cross. The attitude of repentance, brokenness and faith opens the way for the strengthening of the ties of this new relationship even though it does not reach the ideal state in this life. Christians recognize that, rightfully, Christ is the only true center of life. The very fact that they can afford to accept the fact that they are sinners in not giving Him that place has a tremendous influence for strengthening the ties of fellowship among Christians.

This new relationship is illustrated in I Corinthians 12:14-31 by the human body. Christ is the head of the body, and each member functions in its appropriate place in relation to His headship. Each member of the body does not have a separate life; there is one life for the entire body. No member of the body complains of its position, but each serves in perfect harmony with other members. The function of each member of the body is not determined by majority vote. Each member naturally performs the function for which it is created and there is no dissension. A common headship, to which all submit, makes it possible for the entire body to function as a whole. One life flows through the entire body and the members all participate of the same life.

This is the ideal for the Christian. All Christians are a part of one body of whom Christ is the head. It is God's purpose that they should function as one harmonious unit. This ideal is not achieved in this life, for Christians still are sinners. However, every failure to function in complete harmony under the common headship of Jesus Christ is evidence of sinfulness and should lead to repentance and brokenness.

Paul goes directly from this illustration of the human body to the thirteenth chapter of I Corinthians, which is his great dissertation on Christian love. When we read these two chapters together, we understand that he is saying that love, which is the very essence of God, becomes a unique unifying force, to make this new relationship possible.

The fourth chapter of Ephesians is an example of the kind of appeal which the New Testament makes for ethical living, which is based on this new relationship. Christians are urged to exercise lowliness, meekness, patience, forbearance, and love, not just because of the personal benefits which will result, but because they manifest the Christian's eagerness "to maintain the unity of the Spirit in the bond of peace" (verse 3). Christians are not separate units, each looking to his own benefit. The entire body functions as a unit. "There is one body and one Spirit . . . one hope . . . one Lord, one faith" etc. (verses 4, 5). Within this body of Christians there is a diversity of functions and special gifts, but the purpose even of this diversity is that "we may no longer be children, tossed to and fro and carried about with every wind of doctrine. . . . Rather, speaking the truth in love, we are to grow up in every way into him who is the head, into Christ" (verses 14-15). In other words, the purpose of all the diverse functions within the Christian fellowship is the building up of the entire fellowship into one organic unit of which Christ is the head and life-center.

In this new relationship we should speak the truth, not just because falsehood is wicked, but because "we are members one of another" (verse 25). It is inconceivable that the members of our body would lie to one another. What would happen, for instance, if the teeth flashed a false signal to the tongue before they closed? The tongue would be painfully lacerated and the entire body would suffer. Truthfulness simply must prevail in Christian relationships if the entire body is to function normally. The fact that truthfulness benefits the individual member, or the possibility that it may be painful or embarrassing to an individual to tell the truth are not the primary considerations, for not he, but Christ, is at the center of life. When an individual is restrained by personal embarrassment from telling the truth, he is made to realize that he is still a sinner and he has no other recourse but to glory in the cross of Christ and to rejoice in the privilege of repenting.

Christians should not steal. It is true that stealing is wicked, and the thief is condemned by law. Now, however, there is a higher motive to stop stealing: only the fruit of honest labor can be properly used by Christians "to give to those in need" (verse 28). Stealing should be avoided because it is detrimental to the entire body of Christ.

Profanity, vile humor, slander and all such talk is wrong in itself, but the reason the Christian should refrain from evil talk is that he should limit his speech to "such as is good for edifying, as fits the occasion, that it may impart grace to those who hear" (verse 29). Christians should refrain from evil talk, not just because such talk is unlawful, but because it detracts from the oneness of Christian fellowship. It is motivated by the individual's own interests without consideration for what will strengthen the Christian fellowship.

Conduct for the Christian is not determined by such nebulous questions as, "Is it right?" or "Is it wrong?" or "What's wrong with it?" The Christian considers it from this viewpoint: Does it strengthen the spiritual unity among Christians? Does it make life to revolve around Jesus Christ? Does it build us up together in a closer organic relationship with Jesus Christ? If it does these things it should be encouraged. On the other hand, if it represents life as revolving around self, if it tears down our spiritual fellowship with other Christians, if it strains our organic union with Christ, we should refrain from it. When we find we have engaged in practices which have these effects, we have no recourse but to turn from them in repentance, claiming God's forgiveness, for they are evidence of the persistence of sin within us and of our need of the cross of Christ. If we are growing spiritually, we will constantly be made conscious of attitudes and actions which are detrimental to the unity of the Spirit. As we recognize them as sin and repent of them, the ties of fellowship with other Christians will become stronger.

The pastor will share with his flock in this relationship, for he, too, is a sinner. From time to time he will find himself, rather than Christ, at the center of his life. Sometimes he may think of himself as being more than a sinner, as being apart from the fellowship rather than sharing in it. All such barriers are evidence that life is revolving around self. When he faces his own sinfulness and comes as he is, Christ will come in and restore the unity between himself and his fellow Christians. This is the cure for the loneliness which sometimes plagues the life of a pastor.

Those who minister in teaching, in missions, in music, in youth, and in other departments are also sinners. Sometimes they tend to think of themselves as something more than sinners, as specialists who are making a particular contribution to something of which they are not fully a part. Life then revolves around themselves or around the success of their particular department and the unity of the entire body suffers. When they begin to repent and to take the place of sinners who need Christ and the ministry of every part of His body as much as anyone else, the oneness of the body is restored in renewed fellowship.

The work of missions, of evangelism, and of personal witnessing is the work of Christ through all His people. It is not a question of the greatness or of the success of some particular individual. "I planted, Apollos watered, but God gave the growth. So neither he who plants nor he who waters is anything, but only God who gives the growth" (I Corinthians 3:6-7).

No person can say, "See what a wonderful worker I have been. Shame on you for not doing as I have done." There are no great Chrsitians. Only Christ is great. A great Christian would be a divisive force. A great Christ is a uniting power. Individual gifts and abilities are used by the Spirit of God, but individuals are not separate units. All work together and what is accomplished is the work of Christ through His people.

Each individual has unique responsibilities. He should not fret himself because he is not doing what someone else is doing. Such fretfulness must be repented of as sin, for it is not centered in Christ. Likewise, every failure to take the place God has given him should be cause for immediate repentance. His particular duty will become apparent to him as he lives in fellowship with God and with other Christians. Through them, through Christian teaching, through his sense of responsibility, and through the opportunities which present themselves to him, God will reveal to him his unique responsibility. What he does in this way will be related to God's great purpose, for it will be God working through him.

In all the world there is no relationship like that which exists among Christians. The Church has been criticized for her factions and for her divisions, for her blindness to spiritual truth, for her false piety and self-righteousness, for her failure to keep the truth alive and relevant to life. No doubt she is deserving of all these criticisms. She is subject to the frailties of her members who are sinners. She has been smothered by paganism, beset by unbelief, divided and confused by disagreement, and diluted by worldliness. That she exists at all in the world today is a miracle.

Hundreds of people can be found who are poor examples of what Christians should be. Some are immature, some are uninstructed, some are confused, and others are outright counterfeits. Yet, by and large, there are no better homes than the homes of the Christians, no better men than Christian men; there are no better women than Christian women; there is no more understanding fellowship in all the world than the fellowship of the Christians.

Christian people do not have special abilities or special moral resources or special cultural advantages. They are ordinary people who are drawn from all walks of life, who have only this in common, that they recognize themselves to be sinners who are trusting only in Jesus Christ and what He has done on the cross for their pardon and release from the dominion of sin. They are united by their recognition that life for all has only one rightful center, which is Christ.

I was quite ill. It was obvious that unless there was some immediate change, I could not continue in the ministry. This, however, was not a matter of concern to me alone. It was shared by the spiritual leaders of my church. My wife and I knelt together one evening with a few of the deacons who committed the matter to God in order that we might await His will. Over the months that followed, I regained my health. For this I am deeply grateful to God, but it was no stupendous miracle. It was a small thing for Him. The real miracle was the sweetness of our fellowship as we prayed together. A laborer, a college president, a contractor, and a craftsman were included in that group. Yet we were not just a group of individuals. We were one—united by Christ Himself. All of us were sinners, totally dependent on Him. The heart-life that flowed through us all was the life of Christ. The same life has united all His people throughout the ages: we were one with them all. The miracle of the ages is that through Him we may share in this unique relationship.

CHAPTER NINE

Jesus is Lord!

JESUS IS LORD to the Christian. Even the Lordship of Jesus, however, goes back to the cross. "And being found in human form he humbled himself and became obedient unto death, even death on a cross. Therefore God has highly exalted him and bestowed on him the name which is above every name, that at the name of Jesus every knee should bow, in heaven and on earth and under the earth, and every tongue confess that Jesus Christ is Lord, to the glory of God the Father" (Philippians 2:8-11).

It is of primary importance that Jesus be the very Son of God. It is important because no one less than the Son of God could die for our sins, but it is also important because the conflict between man and Jesus must be a demonstration of the conflict between man and God. If this Man who died on the cross was not God, then the cross was not God's means of providing redemption from sin. Then there is neither any justification by faith nor peace with God. The relationship between man and God must be demonstrated in the relationship between man and Jesus Christ. This could not be done if Jesus were not God.

One of the most beautiful symbols of the Bible is the symbol of the Lamb in the midst of the throne of God (Revelation 7:17). The Lamb is God, with all His divine attributes, but helpless as a lamb to force men to honor and obey Him. Jesus was the Lamb. His crucifiers did not recognize Him as God, but He had all God's attributes. Therefore, what they did with Him reveals what they would do with God if they dared. In order to establish that men's attitude toward Jesus revealed their true attitude toward God, it was now necessary to declare Jesus to be indeed the Son of God. When Jesus is revealed to be the Son of God, men are revealed to be sinners indeed.

The primary significance of the resurrection of Jesus was to declare Him to be the Son of God. The apostolic preaching emphasized the resurrection of Jesus and it climaxed in the proclamation that He was thereby designated to be both Lord and Christ, and the very Son of God. Paul sets the stage for the entire epistle to the Romans by saying that Christ was "designated Son of God in power according to the Spirit of holiness by his resurrection from the dead" (Romans 1:4). As Peter said, on the Day of Pentecost, "This Jesus God raised up, and of that we all are witnesses. . . . Let all the house of Israel therefore know assuredly that God has made him both Lord and Christ, this Jesus whom you crucified" (Acts 2:32-36).

We must recognize that Jesus is not made Lord by anything we say or do. He has been declared Lord by more worthy lips than ours. Christianity rests, fundamentally, on the Lordship of Jesus, and the Lordship of Jesus rests on more solid ground than our confession. His Lordship as the Son of God was proclaimed by God Himself when He raised Him from the dead. If no man were to accept Him, and all the world were to rebel against Him, Jesus would still be Lord of all.

Confessing Jesus as Lord brings us into conformity with what God has already proclaimed Him to be. It involves the moral issue of whether we will honor God as God. Therefore, we are right back at the cross where the problem of sin is dealt with. Honoring God as God and confessing Jesus as Lord are really the same thing. If we confess Jesus as Lord, God is God to us; if we will not confess Jesus as Lord, then God is not God to us.

It is the Spirit of God who makes it possible for us to accept the Lordship of Jesus. As Paul says, "No one can say 'Jesus is Lord' except by the Holy Spirit" (I Corinthians 12:3). This happens when the Holy Spirit is permitted to reveal to us that, through the cross, God may again be God to us.

Some people think of any rebellion against Jesus as evidence that He is not really their Lord. They think of having first accepted Him as their Saviour; and then they anticipate making Him their Lord by an act of special consecration, which will bring their life into complete subjection to Him. However, the fact that we discover rebellion within us against His authority does not mean that He is not our Lord. In fact, it means just the opposite. How could we rebel against Him if He were *not* our Lord? The very fact that we recognize the rebellion of our human nature against His authority is evidence that we recognize His right to rule over us. We do not make Jesus our Lord by becoming submissive to Him. However, we recognize that because he *is* our Lord, we should, therefore, be submissive to Him. Our rebellion against His lordship only brings us again and again to our need of repentance and the cross.

About one thing we must have no illusions. The Lord, Himself, must always be the Way. I am well aware that someone may find something in this little book that sounds helpful and logical, and may begin to consider it a way to Christ or to closer fellowship with Him. He will then be caught in an intricate pattern of demands for repentance, submission, confession and self-abasement.

This is a tendency among men. God once commanded Moses to hang up a brazen serpent so that those who would look upon it might live. After some time the people turned their backs on God and began to worship the serpent. That which God desires to be an instrument in His hands tends to turn our attention from Christ. Sometimes it is priests, sometimes it is religious specialists, often it is certain Christian principles, and quite often it is books.

This book should definitely not be considered a handbook on abundant living. What a tragedy it would be if anyone should think that plodding through its pages and seeking to comprehend these principles is a way to come closer to Christ. A few of the Biblical passages I have discussed are difficult to interpret. Let no one think that the ability to fathom their depths will make life more abundant for him.

I dare not leave any chance impression that it was these truths which led me to a closer relationship to Christ. As I have already stated, it was because Christ was leading me that the pastures became green. Whatever God has used to bring a blessing to my soul even now becomes dry and stale apart from His continual presence.

Now, I would like to return to my unbelieving friend, with whom I began in the first chapter. He needs the "Good News" of Christ, yet he is lacking in faith and blind to spiritual truth. He has therefore resigned himself to being a lost soul.

We have discovered in these journeys both in the Scriptures and in human experience that it is for just such as he that God sent His Son, Jesus Christ, to die on a certain special cross. On every journey through which these pages have led us, we have seen that we do not need great faith, accomplishments or special abilities or powers of spiritual perception to meet Christ. We may meet Him where we are, simply as sinners.

God is not challenging him to see how righteous and acceptable he can become. He invites him to accept God's verdict that he is the sinner for whom Christ died. He is a sinner, not because of any terrible things he may have done, but because God is not God to him. God will make this clear to him as he sees how Jesus died on the cross for him.

Christ does not expect him to stop being a sinner before He will meet with him. He invites him to come just as he is, with his sin, his blindness, and his unbelief. God is saying that He holds nothing against him, and He invites him to accept His pardon. He does not ask him to come and try to save himself by becoming a better man. He invites him to come, facing the full extent of his sin, and to accept Christ's promise that He will save him.

When this little book has been used to show him that Christ is all he needs, and to persuade him to come as he is to Him, it will have served its purpose. Beyond this point it is best if it fades into insignificance so that nothing will stand between him and the crucified Christ whom he now meets for the first time.

I would also like to return to the little circle of believing friends who were with me in the first chapter. Lacking in faith to go on to higher things in the Christian life, they are at the point of despair. To these burdened, distressed and weary souls who labor under spiritual bondage, Jesus is immediately available. He waits to meet them just where they are and to lead them to the green pastures. However, they themselves must never expect to look upon themselves as anything more than sinners. They may walk with Jesus only as they recognize that they must constantly trust in His pardon and grace.

When they have seen these things, this book will have served its purpose for them also. It will then be best for them if they turn their attention directly to Christ, so that no set of principles or formulas will take the place of His living presence.

The right of Jesus to rule over all creation gives a larger perspective to life. First life revolved around ourselves. Then, when we were captivated by the cross, we saw that it was sinful for life to revolve around ourselves, that God must be the center. Now, still in the light of the cross, our vision is enlarged to see the great purpose of God, "that at the name of Jesus every knee should bow." We can no longer be satisfied to live unto ourselves. Though God is infinitely concerned about our individual needs, each of us is only a tiny atom in His great purpose. We become lost in the glory of the majestic Lordship of Jesus, and the most natural response is to present ourselves, in an act of worship, to be His servants.

He is our Lord, and life rightfully revolves only around Him. It has no other true center. Yet, even in the glory of His lordship, there will never be anything more glorious about Him than the fact that He died for us. As our perspective enlarges, our need of the cross grows, for the constant insistence of our rebellious natures that life should revolve around ourselves becomes, in the light of the magnitude of God's purpose, more sinful than ever before. Whether we meet Christ now for the first time, or whether we are already walking with Him, there is nothing we need more than the benefits of His death on the cross for sinners. This is God's doing. It is when He captivates us that life begins for us.

> *For from him and through him and to him*
> *are all things. To him be glory forever.*
> *Amen.*

THE END

Fruits to Kay and Roberta
Call Cal
Call Dave about House
Call mike about Devon
2nd atomizer